THE IN-BETWEEN BUDGET

Managing Money When a Household Suddenly Has One Income

by Felix N.BBA.MA.

— A field guide to the space between two incomes —

This book is a work of original, independently developed non-fiction. The households and specific incidents described throughout are composites built from recurring patterns across households navigating an unchosen income gap; they are not factual accounts of identifiable individuals or families. See "A Note on the Households in These Pages" in the back matter.

First edition 2026.

CONTENTS

FRONT MATTER

How to Use This Book

This is not a book about how to find a new job. It is not a book about choosing to live on one income by design, the way some households deliberately do to raise children or simplify a life. It is a book about the specific, disorienting middle stretch that opens the moment a second income stops arriving without anyone in the household choosing it — the layoff, the sudden end of a contract, the small company that closes its doors on a Tuesday — and closes again, eventually, when income returns. That middle stretch is what this book calls the in-between, and almost nothing written about money is built for it.

Most personal finance advice assumes one of two starting points: a household with two stable incomes trying to optimize what it already has, or a household committing to permanent single-income living as a lifestyle choice, with time to plan the transition in advance. Neither describes what actually happens on the afternoon a phone call or a termination letter changes your household's math with no warning and no clear end date. This book was built for that afternoon, and for the weeks and months that follow it.

The book is organized in five parts. Part One helps you get your bearings in the first hours and days, when the instinct to either freeze or build a perfect spreadsheet are both, in their own ways, unhelpful. Part Two introduces the Bridge Method, the framework this book uses in place of a rigid financial blueprint — four things a household needs to hold steady across an uncertain gap, and one honest habit that keeps them accurate. Part Three is the action engine: the specific, practical chapters on bills, renegotiation, housing, coverage, side income, and the people in your life who can actually help, once you tell them the truth. Part Four addresses what happens when the bridge runs longer than expected, or when the people crossing it together start to strain against each other. Part Five is about reaching the other side — what changes when income returns, and what you carry forward from this stretch so that the next gap, if one ever comes, is smaller and easier to cross.

Every chapter ends with a short section called "This Week's Crossing" — two or three concrete actions sized to fit into a week that is already harder than most weeks, not a fresh list of homework on top of an already overwhelming situation. You do not need to complete every action in every chapter before moving to the next one. You need to do the two or three that apply to your actual household this week, and come back to the rest later if they still matter once you do.

A note on the households described throughout this book: Naomi and Theo, Imani and Sam, Ruth, Tobias, Zoe and Malik, and Corinne and Dev are composites, built from patterns that repeat constantly across households facing an unchosen income loss. None of them is a specific real person, and the full explanation of why this book uses composites rather than named case studies appears in the back matter, in "A Note on the Households in These Pages."

If you are reading this in the first forty-eight hours after the news, you have permission to skip straight to Part One and come back for this introduction later. Getting your footing matters more right now than reading in order.

Introduction: The Space Between Two Incomes

There is a particular kind of math that only exists in the space between two incomes, and almost no one teaches it, because almost no one plans to need it. It is not the math of building wealth over decades, and it is not the math of living well within a stable, known budget. It is faster, more urgent, and more forgiving of imperfection than either of those — the math of getting a household safely across a gap of unknown width, using whatever is actually on hand, starting today.

If a job has just ended, or a contract has just quietly not been renewed, or a small business that used to bring in a second income has just closed its doors, you are standing at the edge of that gap right now, and you likely feel two contradictory pulls at once. One is the pull toward total inaction — a kind of financial freeze, where the size of the uncertainty makes even opening a banking app feel like more than you can manage today. The other is the pull toward a different kind of unhelpful response: building an elaborate, color-coded, twelve-tab spreadsheet that tries to account for every possible outcome before you've had a single full night of sleep since the news arrived. Both responses come from the same honest place — the sudden loss of a second income is genuinely destabilizing, and your instincts are trying to restore a sense of control as fast as possible. Neither one, on its own, gets you where you need to go.

This book offers a third path, built around a single idea that shapes everything that follows: you do not need a blueprint for a permanent new life. You need a bridge across a specific gap, engineered for the actual distance you're crossing, checked regularly, and taken down once you've reached the other side. A blueprint assumes you know the final shape of things and are building for good. A bridge assumes you don't yet know exactly how wide the gap is, and it is engineered to hold anyway — sized to the actual weight it needs to carry, inspected on a rhythm, adjusted as the real distance becomes clearer. That distinction — bridge, not blueprint — is the mantra this book keeps returning to, because it changes the kind of planning that feels appropriate. You are not failing at long-term financial planning right now. You are doing a different, narrower, more urgent kind of work, and it deserves its own method rather than a scaled-down version of advice built for a different problem.

The chapters ahead walk through that method in the order most households actually need it: stabilize first, understand the real shape of the gap second, then work through the practical weight the household is carrying — the bills, the housing question, the coverage gap, the honest conversations — before turning to what happens when the crossing takes longer than planned, and finally to what it looks like to reach the other side with the household, and the relationships inside it, intact.

One last thing before Part One begins. Nothing in this book asks you to feel calm about an income loss you didn't choose. It asks you to make a smaller number of better decisions than panic would produce on its own, using a method built specifically for the ground you're standing on right now — not the ground you'll be standing on once this is over.

~

PART ONE: THE DIAGNOSTIC

~

Chapter 1: The Day the Second Paycheque Stopped

Naomi found out on a Tuesday, in a video call that lasted four minutes, that the logistics company where Theo had worked for six years was closing its regional office by the end of the month. Theo called her from the parking lot before he'd even driven home. She remembers the specific, useless thought that arrived first: they had just repainted the kitchen. Not the mortgage, not the two kids' school fees, not the number sitting in their joint chequing account — the kitchen, freshly painted a colour they'd debated for weeks, suddenly felt like evidence of a household that hadn't seen this coming, which was true, and which didn't matter at all, and which she thought about anyway for the rest of that day.

This is worth naming directly, before any practical advice arrives: an unchosen income loss produces a specific kind of disorientation that has almost nothing to do with the size of the number involved. Households with substantial savings and households with almost none report strikingly similar first-day experiences — a kind of static that makes ordinary thinking difficult, paired with an urge to either do everything at once or do nothing at all. If that's where you are right now, reading this on the day the news arrived or in the first few days after, the static is not a sign you're handling this badly. It's a normal, temporary response to a genuine shock, and it usually clears enough within a few days for clearer decisions to become possible.

What actually needs to happen today, versus what can wait

The instinct, once the initial static clears even slightly, is often to try to solve the entire problem immediately — recalculate the whole household budget, contact every biller, decide whether to move, all in the same afternoon. This instinct is understandable and almost always counterproductive, because a full financial picture built in a state of shock tends to be either wildly pessimistic or artificially optimistic, and either version makes the decisions that follow worse. What actually needs attention on day one is much narrower: confirming the exact date the income stops (not the date of the news, which are often different), locating any severance, notice pay, or final payment details in writing, and pausing any large, discretionary, or easily reversible spending until a clearer picture exists. That's the entire list. Everything else in this chapter, and in the two that follow it, can legitimately wait a few more days.

The difference between the news and the number

There's a specific confusion worth untangling early, because it drives a lot of unnecessary panic: the emotional size of the news and the financial size of the problem are not the same measurement, and treating them as identical produces decisions sized to the wrong thing. A household with three months of expenses already set aside and modest fixed costs is in a meaningfully different financial position than a household living paycheque to paycheque with significant debt, even if the emotional experience of the news lands with equal force in both homes. Chapter Two builds the actual financial picture — the real number, distinct from the size of the shock. For today, it's enough to notice that the two are different, and that most of the fear in the first forty-eight hours is responding to the news itself rather than to a number anyone has actually calculated yet.

Who to tell today, and who can wait

Naomi and Theo made one decision well in that first week, almost by accident: they told their two kids something true and age-appropriate that same evening — that Dad's job had ended, that they were going to figure out the plan together as a family, and that nothing about school or the routine was changing this week — and they told almost no one else for several more days. This turned out to be close to the right instinct. Immediate family living in the household benefits from early, honest, calm information, partly because children in particular tend to fill an information gap with something worse than the truth if left to guess. Wider disclosure — extended family, friends, professional networks — is worth handling more deliberately, and Chapter Fourteen covers exactly how to do that well. There's no need to decide the full disclosure question on day one; there is a need to have one honest conversation with the people who live in the house.

The one framework decision that matters this week

Everything in this book builds toward a single reframing, introduced properly in Chapter Four: you are not building a permanent new financial life starting today. You are building a bridge across a gap of currently unknown width, and a bridge doesn't need to account for every possible future — it needs to hold for the actual distance, checked and adjusted as that distance becomes clearer. Holding onto that distinction now, even loosely, can quiet some of the pressure to have every answer immediately. You don't need the blueprint for the rest of your life this week.

You need the first few footings of a bridge, and those are covered in the next chapter.

If the news came as a slow leak rather than a single call

Not every income loss arrives in one clean moment the way Theo's did. Some households watch a slower unraveling — reduced hours that keep shrinking, a small business's revenue that keeps declining month over month before finally becoming unworkable, a series of "just a few more weeks" updates from an employer in obvious trouble that eventually end in closure. If your own situation looked more like this than a single defining phone call, the same first-day guidance still applies, just anchored to a different marker: rather than "the day the news arrived," use the day it became clear the second income had genuinely, functionally stopped, and start this chapter's list from there, even if that date feels less dramatic or less clean than a single Tuesday-afternoon call.

Give yourself the rest of today

One last permission worth stating plainly: nothing in this chapter needs to happen in the first few hours. Confirming dates, gathering paperwork, pausing discretionary spending, and having one honest conversation with the household can all reasonably wait until tomorrow if today is simply too much. What matters more than speed on day one is not making the specific mistakes covered in the chapters ahead — a large, irreversible decision made in shock, a bill quietly missed because no one was tracking it, a child left to guess at a truth no one told them. Beyond avoiding those, there's no prize for moving fast on the worst day of a difficult stretch.

This Week's Crossing

- Confirm the exact date the income stops and get any severance, notice pay, or final payment terms in writing, even if it's just an email confirming what was said out loud.
- Pause discretionary and easily reversible spending for the next week while a clearer picture comes together — this is a pause, not a permanent decision.
- Have one honest, age-appropriate conversation with everyone currently living in the household before the day ends.

Chapter 2: Emergency Math, Not Perfect Math

A household's first real financial task after an income loss is not a monthly budget. It's a forty-eight-hour triage number — a fast, deliberately rough calculation whose only job is to answer one question: how much room does this household actually have before something urgent has to change? A monthly budget, built properly, takes real time, accounts for irregular expenses, and benefits from a clear head. Almost no one has a clear head in the first two days, and waiting for one before doing any math at all leaves a household flying blind through the exact window when a few fast decisions matter most. Emergency math solves a different, narrower problem than a monthly budget does, and it's worth understanding that difference before starting, so the inevitable rough edges don't feel like a failure.

The three numbers that make up triage math

Emergency math needs exactly three inputs, each of which can be found within an hour by almost any household, using whatever records are already on hand — a banking app, a folder of bills, a rough memory of the mortgage or rent payment. The first is cash on hand: everything sitting in chequing and savings accounts that could reasonably be used, added together into one number. The second is committed monthly outflow: the total of housing, minimum debt payments, insurance, utilities, and any other bill that arrives on a fixed schedule regardless of what else is happening, added together into a second single number. The third is incoming money still expected in the near term — a final paycheque, a severance payment, any benefit already confirmed — kept as a separate figure rather than folded into cash on hand, since it usually arrives on a different timeline. Nothing else belongs in this calculation yet. Groceries, discretionary spending, and every other variable cost get handled properly in Chapter Four's Footings work; triage math is deliberately narrower than that.

Turning three numbers into one honest sentence

Once those three figures exist, they combine into a single sentence that becomes the household's true starting point: "We have [cash on hand] plus [incoming money], and our committed costs are [monthly outflow], which gives us roughly [X] weeks before we need to make a bigger decision." Zoe and Malik did this calculation on their kitchen table two days after Malik's position was eliminated, using a phone calculator and the back of an envelope, and arrived at just under eleven weeks — a number that felt smaller than they'd hoped and considerably less catastrophic than the vague dread they'd been carrying since the news. The number itself matters less, at this stage, than the fact that it exists. A known number, even an uncomfortable one, is something a household can plan around. An unknown one is something a household can only fear.

Why rough is the right level of precision here

There's a strong pull, particularly for detail-oriented people, to make this calculation more precise than it needs to be — tracking down the exact interest accrual on a credit card balance, accounting for a rebate that might arrive in six weeks, adjusting for a bill that fluctuates seasonally. Precision at this level costs real time during the exact window when speed matters more, and it creates a false sense that the number is more fixed than it actually is. Triage math is meant to be revisited and refined within the next week or two, once the shock has settled and Chapter Four's fuller Footings work happens. Its job right now is simply to replace "we don't know" with "roughly this many weeks," which is a large and useful improvement even at rough precision.

What the number is for, and what it isn't for

The triage number exists to answer one specific question honestly — how much immediate runway does this household have — and it should not be treated as a verdict on the household's broader financial health, its past choices, or its long-term prospects. A short runway number is genuinely useful information: it tells a household to accelerate certain decisions, covered throughout Part Three, sooner rather than later. It is not evidence of failure, and treating it that way tends to produce shame-driven decisions rather than clear ones. Tobias, whose freelance income had dried up when his primary client ended their contract with almost no warning, found his triage number came out to just under four weeks, and spent an uncomfortable evening treating that number as proof he'd mismanaged his finances for years. The number wasn't a verdict. It was information, and the households that use it well are the ones who can hold it as information rather than as judgment.

Doing this calculation together, if there's a "together" to do it with

For households with more than one adult, this first calculation is worth doing side by side rather than separately, even though it's tempting for one partner to simply handle it alone and report the result. Sitting down together to add up the same three numbers, even briefly, means both people start from the same shared reality rather than two separate private estimates — one of which is often quietly more pessimistic than the other. Chapter Eight covers what happens when partners bring different fears and assumptions to money conversations in more depth; for now, it's enough to notice that the triage number is more useful, and less likely to become a source of later conflict, when it's calculated together rather than delivered.

If the number comes out worse than you feared

Occasionally, a household's honest triage number comes out shorter than even a pessimistic guess anticipated, and it's worth naming directly what that does and doesn't mean. A short runway number means several of this book's later chapters — the renegotiation work in Chapter Six, the income-support mapping in Chapter Seven, the no-severance guidance in Chapter Nineteen if it applies — deserve immediate, this-week attention rather than the more measured pace a longer runway might allow. It does not mean the situation is unsalvageable, and it does not mean the household has run out of options; it means the sequence of decisions in this book needs to move faster, which is genuinely different information than "there's nothing to be done," however similar the two might feel in the first wave of seeing an uncomfortably small number.

This Week's Crossing

- Calculate the three triage numbers — cash on hand, committed monthly outflow, and confirmed incoming money — using rough figures from memory or a quick account check.

- Turn those three numbers into the one-sentence runway statement, and write it down somewhere you'll actually see it again.
- If there's more than one adult in the household, do this calculation together rather than separately, even if it takes an extra twenty minutes to coordinate.

Chapter 3: The Cost of "Temporary"

The single word that causes the most financial damage during an income gap isn't a number or a bill. It's the word "temporary," used as a reason to delay decisions that would actually help. "This is temporary, so there's no point restructuring anything." "This is temporary, so we'll just put it on the card for now." "This is temporary, so I don't want to make a big deal out of asking for help." Each of these sentences sounds reasonable in the moment, and each one quietly assumes something no household in this position can actually know: exactly how long the gap will last. Treating an unknown timeline as a reason to delay is one of the most common and most avoidable mistakes covered in this book, and this chapter exists to replace that instinct with a better one.

Why "temporary" feels safer than it is

There's a real emotional logic behind the delay instinct, and it's worth naming honestly rather than dismissing. Making a change — renegotiating a bill, adjusting a budget, having a hard conversation with a partner — can feel like an admission that the situation is serious enough to require action, which is uncomfortable when part of you is still hoping the gap closes quickly. Waiting feels, briefly, like optimism. In practice, waiting on the assumption of a short timeline usually means the response scales up in a rush once the timeline turns out to be longer than hoped, at exactly the point when the household has less runway and more accumulated strain to work with. The households that manage an income gap best aren't the ones who predict its length correctly — almost no one does — they're the ones who build a plan that works reasonably well whether the gap turns out to be four weeks or four months.

Budgeting for a range, not a guess

The practical fix for this is simpler than it sounds: instead of picking a single guessed timeline and building a plan around it, build a plan around a range, and check back against reality on a fixed schedule rather than waiting for certainty that may never arrive. A useful range for most households, absent better information, spans a shorter estimate — a month or two, matching typical severance or notice periods — and a longer one, several months out, sized to what the household's actual runway from Chapter Two could realistically stretch to cover if it had to. The plan doesn't need to solve for the longer end of that range today. It needs to acknowledge the range exists, so that decisions made this week don't quietly assume the shorter, more comfortable end is guaranteed.

The specific decisions that shouldn't wait for certainty

A short list of decisions consistently benefits from happening early rather than being delayed on the hope of a quick resolution, precisely because they either cost little to start now or cost considerably more the longer they're delayed. Renegotiating recurring bills, covered fully in Chapter Six, costs almost nothing to attempt and produces savings starting immediately once it succeeds — waiting a month to try it is a month of savings simply not collected. Reviewing insurance and benefit coverage gaps, covered in Chapter Thirteen, matters more the longer a gap runs, not less, since coverage that quietly lapses is far easier to prevent than to fix retroactively. Having an honest conversation with a partner about shared expectations, covered in Chapter Eight, becomes harder the longer it's avoided, not easier, since unspoken assumptions tend to calcify into resentment when left unaddressed. None of these decisions require knowing the gap's true length. All of them get more expensive, in money or in strain, the longer "temporary" is used as a reason to wait.

What "temporary" gets right, and how to keep that part

None of this means treating the gap as permanent, which carries its own real costs — a household that restructures its entire life around an assumption of long-term single income when the gap turns out to be six weeks has spent real energy solving a problem it didn't actually have. The useful version of "temporary" isn't "so there's no need to act," it's "so the actions we take should stay reversible where possible." Renegotiating a bill down is reversible. Taking on a manageable bridge-income project, covered in Chapter Eleven, is reversible. Selling a car or breaking a lease is much less reversible, and decisions in that category deserve more deliberation and, usually, more time before committing, precisely because "temporary" turning out to be accurate would mean an unnecessary, hard-to-undo cost.

Ruth's month that became five

Ruth, let go from a corporate role after twenty-two years during a restructuring, told herself for the first several weeks that she'd have something new within a month — a reasonable hope, given her experience, that turned out not to match her actual timeline, which stretched past five months before a new position came through. What made the difference for Ruth wasn't predicting the longer timeline correctly early on; she didn't. It was that she'd made her early decisions — renegotiating her car insurance, confirming her health coverage options, having a clear conversation with her adult children about the situation — in a way that held up regardless of how long the gap actually turned out to be, rather than betting everything on the one-month guess being right. When month two arrived and the job search was still open, she wasn't starting those decisions from scratch under more pressure. She was simply continuing a plan already built to handle exactly this.

Hope without denial

None of this chapter's argument is against hope — a household that genuinely expects a shorter gap and turns out to be right hasn't done anything wrong by hoping. The distinction that matters is between hope as an emotional stance, which is healthy and worth keeping, and hope as the actual basis for financial planning, which is where the trouble starts. Zoe found a version of this that worked well for her household: she allowed herself to genuinely believe Malik's search would go quickly, while still building the household's actual plan around the wider range, treating the two as separate and not letting the emotional hope quietly substitute for the more cautious planning underneath it.

Revisiting the range as real information arrives

The timeline range described in this chapter isn't meant to be set once and forgotten — it should tighten as real information arrives, whether that's an interview that suggests things are moving quickly, or a stretch of silence that suggests the longer end of the range deserves more weight. Treating the range as a living estimate, updated honestly at each Bridge Reading rather than defended out of a wish for the original guess to be right, keeps the whole household's planning grounded in the clearest available picture rather than an increasingly outdated first impression.

This Week's Crossing

- Write down both ends of your household's realistic timeline range — a shorter estimate and a longer one — rather than committing to a single guessed number.
- Identify one decision you've been delaying "because this is temporary," and ask honestly whether waiting is actually saving you anything or simply postponing a cost.
- Prioritize reversible actions first — renegotiating bills, reviewing coverage, having honest conversations — over larger, harder-to-undo decisions, until the timeline becomes clearer.

~

PART TWO: THE BRIDGE METHOD

~

Chapter 4: The Bridge, Not the Blueprint

Every household that has ever tried to plan its way through an income gap eventually runs into the same design problem, whether or not anyone names it directly: how do you plan carefully for a distance you can't yet measure? A blueprint doesn't answer that question well, because a blueprint assumes a known, final shape — the complete floor plan of a building, drawn before the first wall goes up, built for permanence. An income gap isn't a building. It's a specific, bounded distance between two points — the day the second income stopped, and the day it starts again — and what a household actually needs is something engineered for a gap, not a structure built for good. That's the idea behind this book's method, and it's worth spending a full chapter on before moving into the practical work of Part Three, because the shape of the method changes how every later decision gets made.

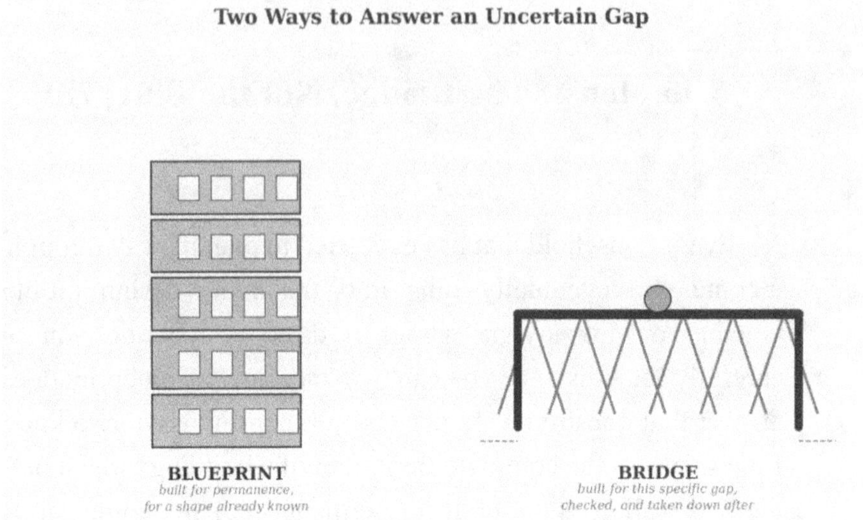

Two ways to answer an uncertain gap: a blueprint built for permanence, or a bridge sized to the actual distance.

Why a bridge is a better model than a blueprint

A bridge is built to solve one specific problem: get load safely across a gap, sized to the actual distance and the actual weight it needs to carry, for as long as that gap exists. Bridge engineers don't design for every conceivable future use of the crossing — they design for the crossing that's actually needed, inspect it on a regular schedule once it's built, and adjust or reinforce it as conditions change. That's a meaningfully different posture than a blueprint's assumption of permanence, and it maps unusually well onto an income gap. You don't need to redesign your entire financial life for a future that may or may not arrive. You need a structure sized to get your household across this specific stretch, checked regularly, and taken down — deliberately, not by accident — once you've reached the other side. Chapter Twenty-

Three returns to exactly that dismantling, once income has returned.

The four things every bridge needs, translated to a household

A structurally sound bridge rests on four things, and each one has a direct household equivalent that this book uses as its organizing framework for the chapters ahead. Footings are the stable base a bridge is built on — the immediate, non-negotiable stabilization work covered in Chapters One through Three, and refined further in this chapter's own closing section. Span is the measured distance the bridge needs to cross — the honest, range-based timeline work from Chapter Three, and the runway mapping that Chapter Seven builds out fully using severance and benefits. Load is everything the bridge actually has to carry day to day — the bills, debts, housing decisions, coverage gaps, and income options that make up most of Part Three. Crossing is the people making their way across together — the partner alignment, the children's stability, and the honest disclosure to a wider network that Chapters Eight, Nine, and Thirteen cover in turn. Every chapter from here forward sits under one of these four categories, and knowing which one you're working on at any given moment makes the whole method easier to hold in your head without a spreadsheet in front of you.

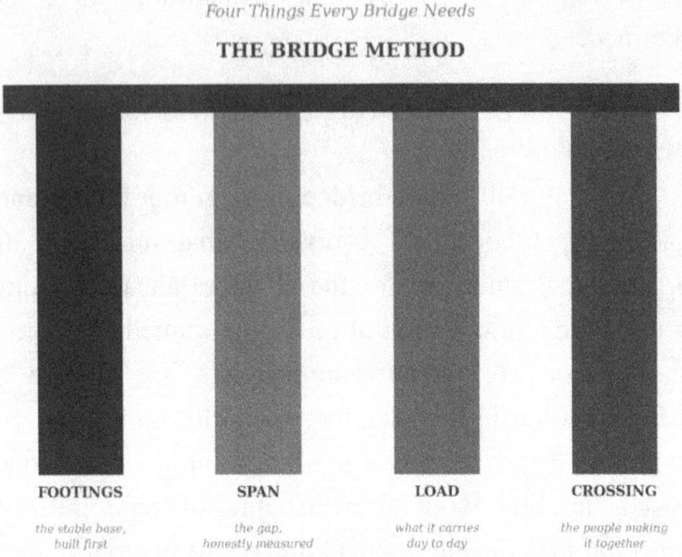

The Bridge Method's four pillars: Footings, Span, Load, and Crossing.

Footings: what "stable base" actually means here

Footings, in practical terms, means the household's core stabilization work is genuinely done, not just started — the triage number from Chapter Two is calculated and revisited with real figures rather than rough guesses, the timeline range from Chapter Three is written down, and the initial pause on discretionary spending has either continued deliberately or been lifted deliberately, rather than simply drifting back to normal without anyone deciding that. Naomi and Theo spent their first full weekend after the layoff finishing this step properly — pulling actual account statements rather than estimating from memory, and writing their range on a sticky note on the refrigerator where both of them, and eventually their kids, would see it. That sticky note stayed up for the better part of three months, and Naomi later said its presence did more to reduce the household's background anxiety than any single financial decision they made, simply because the range was visible and shared rather than something each of them was quietly guessing at alone.

The Bridge Reading: the habit that replaces one big plan

A bridge built once and never inspected again is a bridge nobody trusts, no matter how well it was engineered on day one. The same is true of a household plan built once in a moment of shock and never revisited — it either goes stale as circumstances shift, or it quietly stops being followed because nobody checks whether it's still accurate. This book's answer to that problem is a short, recurring practice called the Bridge Reading: fifteen minutes, on a fixed schedule, checking the same core numbers against where they stood last time and making one small adjustment if something has shifted. In the earliest, most volatile weeks of a gap, a weekly Bridge Reading works best, since conditions are changing quickly enough that a monthly check would miss too much. Once a household has genuinely stabilized — usually somewhere around the four-to-six-week mark, though this varies — a monthly rhythm, detailed fully in Chapter Fifteen, takes over. The specific schedule matters less than the principle: small, regular, honest checks beat one large plan built once and trusted blindly for months.

The one test for whether an idea belongs in your bridge

As the chapters ahead introduce specific tactics — renegotiation scripts, savings-order decisions, side-income options — it helps to have one filter for deciding what actually belongs in your household's plan and what's simply reasonable-sounding advice that doesn't fit your actual gap. Ask two questions of anything you're considering adding: does it address a specific, real weight your household is currently carrying, and does it stay appropriately sized to a gap of unknown but probably not permanent length? An idea that passes both tests belongs in your bridge. An idea that fails either one — solving a problem you don't actually have, or committing to something so large it only makes sense as a permanent life change — is worth setting aside until, and unless, the situation genuinely calls for it.

This Week's Crossing

- Revisit your triage number and timeline range from Chapters Two and Three using real account figures rather than estimates, and write the range somewhere visible to the whole household.
- Decide, deliberately, whether your household is in weekly or monthly Bridge Reading territory right now, based on how volatile the situation still feels.
- Run one financial idea you've been considering through the two-question test — does it address a real weight, and does it stay appropriately sized — before committing to it.

Chapter 5: Bills That Didn't Get the Memo

Every household's bills keep arriving on the same schedule they always have, entirely indifferent to the fact that a second income just stopped, and the gap between "our income changed" and "our bills noticed" is where a lot of unnecessary damage happens — not because any single bill is unmanageable, but because nobody has taken a clear, complete inventory of what's actually coming due, so decisions get made bill by bill, in a rush, in whatever order the mail happens to arrive. This chapter is about doing that inventory once, properly, so that every later decision in this book — renegotiation in Chapter Six, savings order in Chapter Ten, housing in Chapter Twelve — starts from an accurate picture rather than a partial one.

Why a bill-by-bill approach fails, and a full inventory doesn't

The instinct to handle bills as they arrive, reactively, feels manageable in the moment — open the envelope or the notification, decide whether to pay it, move to the next one — but it hides the household's total exposure until the end of the month, by which point several decisions have often already been made that a fuller picture would have changed. Imani and Sam discovered this the hard way in their second week after Sam's parental leave turned into a longer gap when his position was eliminated during the leave: they'd paid two subscription renewals and a car insurance premium in full, reactively, before sitting down to build a complete list, only to realize once the full picture existed that one of those subscriptions could have been paused entirely and the insurance premium had a lower-cost option they hadn't known to ask about. A complete inventory, built once, prevents exactly this kind of reactive, information-poor decision-making.

Building the inventory: five categories, one list

A useful household bill inventory sorts every recurring cost into five categories, and the sorting itself does most of the work of clarifying priorities. Housing includes rent or mortgage, property tax if paid separately, and any mandatory condo or association fees. Debt includes every minimum payment on every credit card, loan, or line of credit, listed individually rather than as one lump sum, since Chapter Six's renegotiation work happens creditor by creditor. Insurance includes every policy — home, auto, life, and any health-related coverage not provided through the lost employment, which Chapter Thirteen covers in more depth. Utilities includes the genuinely necessary recurring services — electricity, water, heat, basic phone and internet — distinct from the fifth category. Subscriptions and discretionary recurring costs includes everything else: streaming services, memberships, subscription boxes, anything that recurs on a schedule but isn't strictly necessary to keep the household running. Building this list completely, in one sitting, using actual statements rather than memory, typically takes under an hour and consistently surfaces at least one forgotten or underestimated cost.

What the inventory reveals that memory alone doesn't

Almost every household that builds this inventory carefully finds something they'd underestimated or genuinely forgotten —

a small subscription charged annually rather than monthly, so it doesn't appear in a mental tally of "monthly bills," or an insurance premium that increased at the last renewal without much notice. Corinne, three weeks into a gap after her position at a small nonprofit was eliminated with no severance, found two subscriptions during her inventory that she and her partner Dev had both assumed the other person had already cancelled months earlier — a small discovery, financially, but one that prompted a more useful conversation about how the two of them tracked shared recurring costs generally, a theme Chapter Eight returns to directly.

Sorting the list by what can move and what can't

Once the full inventory exists, the next useful step is marking each item with a rough sense of its flexibility — not yet deciding what to actually do, just noting what category of decision applies. Some costs are essentially fixed in the short term: a mortgage payment doesn't have much room to move without a much larger housing decision, covered in Chapter Twelve. Some costs are negotiable without changing the underlying service, which Chapter Six covers directly — many insurance premiums, some debt terms, and certain utility arrangements have more flexibility than most households assume. Some costs are simply removable, at least temporarily, without much disruption — this is usually where most of the subscriptions and discretionary recurring category ends up. Sorting the list this way, even roughly, turns a single overwhelming total into three smaller, more workable categories, and makes the next two chapters considerably easier to act on.

Keeping the list current, not just building it once

An inventory built once in week one and never updated again slowly drifts out of accuracy — a renegotiated bill changes, a cancelled subscription's final charge still shows up once more before it fully stops, a new cost appears that wasn't there before. The inventory belongs inside the Bridge Reading rhythm introduced in Chapter Four, checked briefly at the same time as the household's core numbers, rather than treated as a one-time project that's finished and filed away. Households that keep this list current report far less of the low-grade dread that comes from a vague sense that "something's probably being missed," because the list itself becomes the answer to that worry rather than leaving it unanswered.

Annual and irregular bills deserve their own line

A complete inventory should also capture costs that don't arrive monthly at all — an annual insurance renewal, a quarterly tax installment, a membership that bills once a year. These are easy to miss entirely when working from a mental list of "monthly bills," and they have a habit of arriving as an unwelcome surprise precisely because so much attention during a gap goes toward the recurring monthly rhythm. Converting each irregular bill into a rough monthly equivalent — dividing an annual cost by twelve, for instance — and adding that figure to the inventory gives a more honest picture of the household's true ongoing obligation than the monthly bills alone would suggest.

Whose name is on what

For partnered households, it's worth noting during the inventory which accounts are held jointly and which are held in only one partner's name, since this affects both the renegotiation conversations in Chapter Six, which generally need to happen with the account holder specifically, and the credit considerations in Chapter Twenty-Two, which apply individually rather than jointly for single-name accounts. A quick notation column on the inventory — whose name, on which account — saves real confusion later, when a call to a lender stalls because the person calling isn't listed as an authorized party on that specific account.

This Week's Crossing

- Build the complete five-category bill inventory in one sitting, using actual statements rather than memory, even if it takes the better part of an hour.
- Mark each item as fixed, negotiable, or removable, without yet deciding what to actually do about any of them.
- Add "check the bill inventory" as a standing item in your household's Bridge Reading, so the list stays accurate rather than going stale.

Chapter 6: Renegotiate Without Shame

Most households have never once called a lender, a landlord, or a service provider to ask for different terms, not because the option doesn't exist, but because asking feels like admitting something uncomfortable out loud to a stranger. That discomfort is real and understandable, and it also costs households real money every month it goes unaddressed, since a striking number of recurring bills have more flexibility built into them than most people realize — flexibility that exists specifically for situations like an income gap, sitting unused simply because nobody asked. This chapter exists to make asking feel ordinary rather than exceptional, with specific language for the conversations that tend to matter most.

Why shame is the wrong frame for this conversation

There's a quiet assumption embedded in how a lot of people think about renegotiation — that asking for adjusted terms signals financial trouble in a way that reflects badly on the household, and that a "responsible" household simply pays what it's billed without asking questions. This assumption doesn't match how these conversations actually work on the other end of the line. Lenders, insurers, and service providers deal with income-disruption requests constantly and generally have standard processes for handling them, precisely because they'd rather adjust terms for a household with a temporary gap than lose a paying customer entirely to default or cancellation. Reframing the call as a normal business conversation — one side has a temporary change in circumstances, the other side has an interest in keeping the relationship rather than losing it — tends to make the actual call considerably easier than the anticipation of it.

The four-part script that works across most conversations

A single flexible structure handles the majority of renegotiation conversations, regardless of who's on the other end: state the situation briefly and factually, without over-explaining or apologizing; state clearly what you're asking for; ask what options exist rather than assuming you already know the full menu; and get anything agreed to in writing before hanging up or ending the chat. In practice, that might sound like: "I wanted to let you know my household's income changed this month due to a layoff. I'm hoping to find a way to keep this account current — what options are available for adjusting the payment or the terms temporarily?" This script works because it's specific enough to be taken seriously, brief enough not to invite an extended personal conversation nobody has the energy for, and it explicitly opens the door for the other side to offer solutions rather than forcing you to guess what to ask for by name.

What tends to be genuinely negotiable

Certain categories of bills consistently have more room than households assume. Insurance premiums — auto, home, sometimes life — often have adjustable payment schedules, coverage-level options, or hardship programs worth asking about directly by name. Credit card and loan payments frequently have hardship or forbearance programs that pause or reduce payments temporarily, usually without the severe credit consequences households fear, though it's worth confirming exactly how any program will be reported before agreeing to it. Utility providers in many regions have income-disruption programs, extended payment plans, or at minimum a willingness to waive a late fee for a household that calls proactively rather than simply missing a payment. Rent is more variable — some landlords have real flexibility, particularly for a tenant with a solid payment history asking early, and some don't — but asking costs nothing and is covered on its own in more depth later in this book's housing chapter.

Calling before you're late, not after

The single factor that most changes how these conversations go is timing: calling proactively, before a payment is missed, puts a household in a fundamentally different negotiating position than calling after a missed payment has already triggered late fees, a ding to a payment history, or an account moving toward collections. Zoe called her auto insurer the same week Malik's layoff was confirmed, well before their next premium was due, and walked away with a temporary reduced-coverage option that saved them close to sixty dollars a month with no gap in the coverage that actually mattered to them. Waiting until the bill was actually overdue would likely have meant a harder conversation, a worse set of options, and a real cost already incurred before the call even started.

Handling a "no" without giving up on the whole category

Not every call produces a helpful answer, and it's worth being prepared for that without treating a single "no" as proof the whole approach doesn't work. If a first representative can't offer anything useful, asking directly whether a supervisor or a specific hardship or retention department exists often surfaces options the first person either didn't know about or wasn't authorized to offer. Tobias, working through his bill inventory after his main client's contract ended, got an unhelpful first answer from his phone provider and a genuinely useful reduced-plan option from the same company's retention line fifteen minutes later, simply by asking who else he could speak with. A "no" from one representative is information about that conversation, not a verdict on the whole request.

Keeping a record as you go

Because these conversations often happen across several calls, sometimes with different representatives at the same company, it's worth keeping a simple running log as you go rather than trusting memory alone — who you spoke with, when, what was offered, and what you agreed to. This isn't just for your own clarity; a documented record gives you something concrete to point to if a promised adjustment doesn't actually appear on the next bill, which happens occasionally simply through administrative error rather than bad faith, and is far easier to resolve quickly with a specific date and representative name in hand than with a vague memory of "someone told me this would be taken care of." The workbook at the end of this book includes a simple template for exactly this log.

Written correspondence as an alternative to a phone call

For anyone who finds a live phone call genuinely difficult, whether from anxiety, a hearing difference, or simply a strong preference for written communication, most of the same requests can be made in writing — an email, a secure message through an online account portal, or a formal letter — using the same four-part structure adapted to written form. Written requests take slightly longer to resolve on average, but they carry a real advantage of their own: a built-in record of exactly what was asked and what was said in response, without needing to keep a separate log at all.

This Week's Crossing

- Pick the two or three bills from your inventory marked "negotiable" that carry the highest monthly cost, and make those calls first.
- Use the four-part script — state, ask, explore options, confirm in writing — for each call, and write down what was agreed to immediately afterward.
- If a first call produces no useful answer, ask specifically about a hardship program, retention department, or supervisor before moving on.

Chapter 7: The Severance and Benefits Bridge

Severance, notice pay, accrued vacation payout, unused benefit balances, and whatever public or employer-provided income support a household may qualify for rarely arrive as one clear, well-explained number on the day a job ends. They arrive scattered — a letter here, a portal login there, a benefits summary buried in an email from months earlier — and most households significantly underestimate either how much total support actually exists or how quickly it will run out, sometimes both at once, simply because nobody has laid every piece out against an actual calendar. This chapter is about building that map properly, since it directly extends the Span work introduced in Chapter Four: knowing the real width of the gap depends on knowing exactly what's coming in, and exactly when.

Gathering every piece before calculating anything

The first step is deliberately unglamorous: collecting every document, portal login, and confirmation email related to severance, notice pay, accrued vacation, and any benefit or income-support program the household might qualify for, before trying to calculate a single number. This matters because pieces are easy to miss when working from memory — an accrued vacation payout that arrives separately from a final paycheque, a small benefits continuation window that wasn't mentioned clearly in the termination conversation, an income-support program with an application window that closes faster than expected if the application isn't started promptly. Wendell, laid off after a company buyout eliminated his department, found during this gathering step that his employer owed him a payout for eleven unused vacation days he hadn't realized had accrued — a genuinely meaningful, easily missed piece of his actual runway that a rushed mental calculation would have left out entirely.

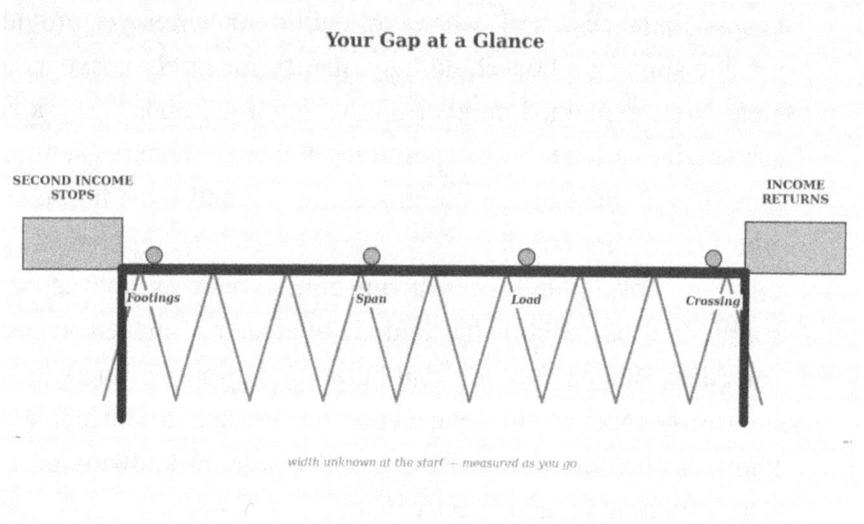

The gap between two incomes, with the four pillars marked along the span.

Mapping every source against an actual calendar

Once every piece is gathered, the useful next step isn't adding everything into one lump total — it's mapping each piece against the specific date it actually arrives, since a household's real cash-flow risk depends as much on timing as on total amount. A severance payment arriving as a lump sum in week two behaves very differently, financially, than the same total amount arriving as continued salary-equivalent payments spread over eight weeks, even though the total is identical — the lump sum creates a larger early cushion and a harder cliff later, while the spread version behaves more like the household's normal income pattern for longer. Building a simple calendar — even a handwritten one, week by week, noting what arrives when — turns a vague sense of "we have some severance coming" into an accurate picture of exactly which weeks are well covered and which weeks need closer attention.

Where households consistently underestimate their runway

Two mistakes show up often enough in this mapping to be worth naming directly. The first is forgetting that some support programs have waiting periods before payments begin, so a program a household is counting on for week one may not actually arrive until week three or four — a gap worth confirming directly with the program rather than assuming. The second is treating gross figures as if they were net, particularly for severance and any taxable income-support payments, which routinely arrive smaller than the headline number once relevant deductions are accounted for. Ruth's initial mental math on her severance overestimated her actual runway by nearly three weeks, entirely because she'd been calculating against the gross figure quoted in her termination letter rather than the smaller number that actually landed in her account — a correction worth making early, since it changes exactly the kind of decisions covered throughout Part Three.

Where households consistently underestimate their support, too

The mistake doesn't only run one direction. Some households, in the disorientation of the first days, don't apply for income-support programs they genuinely qualify for, either because the application felt like more effort than they had energy for that week, or because of a quiet, inaccurate belief that "people like us don't need to ask for that kind of help." Available support that goes unclaimed doesn't make a household's actual gap any narrower — it just means the household is crossing a wider gap than it needs to, using only its own resources when other legitimate support exists. Confirming what's actually available, even when it feels like an unwelcome errand, belongs firmly in this chapter's work rather than being set aside out of discomfort.

Turning the map into an updated Span

Once every source is gathered and mapped against real dates, the household's Span from Chapter Four gets its first real update: instead of a rough range built on early guesswork, there's now an actual calendar showing which weeks are well covered by confirmed income and which weeks currently show a gap. That updated picture feeds directly into the decisions in the chapters ahead — how urgently to pursue bridge income in Chapter Eleven, how to think about savings order in Chapter Ten, and how to weigh housing options in Chapter Twelve. None of those decisions can be made well against a vague sense of "we have some severance." They can be made well against an actual calendar, built once, carefully, using every piece of support the household is genuinely entitled to.

Keeping the map visible, not just accurate

An accurate calendar that lives only in a spreadsheet nobody looks at twice provides less real benefit than a rougher version that's actually visible and referenced regularly. Whatever format a household chooses — a printed calendar on the wall, a shared note, the worksheet in this book's appendix — the goal is a map both adults, where applicable, can glance at and immediately answer "are we on track for this week" without needing to reconstruct the full picture from memory each time. This visibility is part of what keeps the Span accurate over time, since a map nobody looks at is a map nobody notices has gone stale.

When a payment arrives smaller than expected

If a confirmed payment does arrive smaller than the calendar predicted, resist the urge to treat it as evidence the whole plan has failed. A single discrepancy is usually worth a direct follow-up call to confirm whether it was a processing adjustment, a deduction not previously accounted for, or a genuine error, before assuming the worst and rebuilding the entire Span from scratch. Wendell caught exactly this kind of discrepancy in his third week — a payment roughly eight percent smaller than expected — and a single phone call revealed a standard administrative deduction he simply hadn't been told about clearly, resolved with an updated, corrected calendar entry rather than any real cause for alarm.

This Week's Crossing

- Gather every document, login, and confirmation related to severance, vacation payout, and any income-support program, even the pieces that feel minor.
- Build a simple week-by-week calendar showing exactly when each source of income actually arrives, using net rather than gross figures wherever possible.
- Confirm whether you've applied for every income-support program you genuinely qualify for, and if not, treat that application as this week's priority errand.

Chapter 8: One Income, Two Sets of Expectations

Money stress rarely stays contained to money for long in a household with more than one adult in it. It tends to surface as something else first — a sharper tone over a small purchase, a silence after a suggestion that felt dismissed, a disagreement about something apparently unrelated that turns out, on closer inspection, to be about money after all. This happens because partners facing the same income loss often bring genuinely different fears, different instincts about spending, and different unspoken assumptions about what "being careful" actually means in practice — and an income gap has a way of surfacing every one of those differences at once, at exactly the moment the household has the least emotional slack to work through them gently.

Why partners can experience the same event so differently

Two people in the same household, facing the identical loss of income, frequently process it in noticeably different ways, and neither response is wrong on its own. One partner might default to aggressive, immediate cost-cutting — cancelling everything cancellable within the first week — driven by a genuine need to feel some sense of control restored quickly. The other might default to a kind of protective normalcy — resisting visible changes to routines, particularly around kids — driven by an equally genuine instinct to preserve stability during a destabilizing time. Neither instinct is inherently the correct one, and treating a partner's different response as carelessness, or as excessive anxiety, tends to create a second, entirely avoidable conflict layered on top of the first, genuinely difficult situation.

The conversation that needs to happen before the spreadsheet does

Before building a shared budget or agreeing on specific cuts, it helps enormously for partners to have a shorter, more foundational conversation first: what does each of us fear most about this situation, specifically, and what would each of us need to feel like we're handling it well? This conversation isn't about solving anything yet — it's about surfacing the different starting points each partner is quietly working from, so that later, more practical conversations aren't accidentally fighting two different underlying fears without either person naming what they actually are. Corinne and Dev had this conversation on their back porch during their first week, and it surfaced something neither of them had said out loud before: Corinne's biggest fear was that this would define how their families of origin saw her, while Dev's was much more narrowly financial. Once that difference was visible, several later disagreements about specific spending decisions made a lot more sense to both of them, and were easier to resolve.

Building shared agreements, not just a shared spreadsheet

A household budget built jointly is useful, but it solves a narrower problem than partners sometimes expect it to. The budget answers "how much are we spending on what." It doesn't, on its own, answer "who decides when a spending decision falls outside the plan," or "how do we want to handle it if one of us wants to make an exception." Building explicit shared agreements around those questions — a small discretionary amount each partner can spend without a conversation, an agreed process for anything above that amount, a check-in point if either partner feels the plan isn't working — prevents a specific, common source of friction: one partner feeling surveilled over small purchases, and the other feeling blindsided by ones they didn't know about.

When one partner wants to talk about it constantly and the other doesn't

A related mismatch shows up often enough to name directly: partners frequently differ not just in their spending instincts but in how much they want to discuss the situation at all. One partner may find frequent check-ins reassuring; the other may find the same frequency exhausting, experiencing each conversation as a fresh reminder of a stressful situation rather than a helpful update. Neither preference is unreasonable on its own, and the useful fix isn't picking a winner — it's agreeing explicitly on a rhythm that works for both people, which is exactly what the Bridge Reading from Chapter Four is designed to provide: a predictable, bounded, shared check-in on a fixed schedule, rather than either constant informal conversation or an avoidant silence that leaves one partner feeling shut out.

What this looks like when it's working

Naomi and Theo settled, after an uneven first few weeks, into a rhythm where their weekly Bridge Reading became the primary container for money conversations — a fixed fifteen-minute Sunday evening check, with an explicit agreement that either of them could raise something outside that window if it felt urgent, but that most ordinary updates could wait for the scheduled time. This didn't eliminate their disagreements, but it gave those disagreements a predictable, bounded space to happen in, rather than letting money stress leak into every unrelated interaction throughout the week. Chapter Seventeen returns to this territory directly, for households where the mismatch in response styles runs deeper than a simple scheduling fix can resolve.

When one partner handled the money before, and now both need to

In some households, one partner traditionally managed the day-to-day finances while the other stayed less directly involved — not from a lack of interest, but simply from how the division of labor settled over time. An income gap tends to make that arrangement harder to sustain, since the Bridge Reading and the broader Crossing work in this book genuinely benefit from both partners having real, current visibility into the numbers, rather than one partner carrying that knowledge alone while the other absorbs only a summary. This transition can feel awkward at first, and it's worth treating as a skill to build together deliberately, starting with the previously less-involved partner sitting in on a full Bridge Reading from Chapter Fifteen rather than being briefed on its conclusions afterward, until both partners can work through the household's actual numbers with roughly equal confidence.

Checking in on the agreement itself, not just the numbers

It's worth occasionally stepping back from the numbers during a Bridge Reading to ask a slightly different question: is the shared agreement itself still working, or has it quietly become a source of friction in its own right. An agreement that felt fair in week one can start to chafe by week eight if one partner's circumstances have shifted more than the other's — a partner who picked up bridge income covered in Chapter Eleven, for instance, may reasonably want the discretionary-spending agreement revisited. Treating the agreement as adjustable, openly and by mutual consent, tends to keep it durable far longer than treating it as a fixed rule set once and never revisited.

This Week's Crossing

- Have the foundational conversation — what does each partner fear most, and what would help each of you feel like you're handling this well — before building or revising a shared budget.
- Agree explicitly on a small discretionary spending amount each partner can use without a conversation, and a process for anything above it.
- Set a fixed rhythm for money conversations, tied to your Bridge Reading, rather than leaving the frequency of check-ins to chance or to whichever partner brings it up first.

~

PART THREE: THE ACTION ENGINE

~

Chapter 9: Kids, Routines, and the Budget They Don't See

Children absorb far more of a household's financial stress than most parents intend for them to, and they absorb it less through direct conversation than through the ambient signals surrounding them — a tenser tone at dinner, a parent's phone conversation cut short and quiet, a favourite activity that quietly disappears from the calendar without explanation. This chapter is about a specific, achievable balance: making the real budget changes an income gap requires, while protecting the parts of a child's day-to-day routine that matter most to their sense of stability, and being honest with them in a way that's calibrated to their age rather than either full adult detail or total silence.

Why routine matters more to kids than specifics do

Children, especially younger ones, generally register stability through routine and tone far more than through an accurate understanding of household finances, which most kids under a certain age can't fully process anyway. A child who still has the same bedtime, still goes to the same after-school activity, and still experiences their parents as calm and present tends to feel secure even in a household that's quietly cutting costs elsewhere, while a child whose routine changes suddenly and without explanation — even for reasons unrelated to money — can experience real anxiety regardless of how the household's finances are actually doing. This gives parents a genuinely useful piece of leverage:

routine stability and cost reduction aren't nearly as linked as they might first appear, and protecting the first doesn't require abandoning the second.

Finding the cuts that don't touch what matters most

The practical task is identifying which child-related costs can flex without disrupting the routines that actually carry weight for a specific child, since this varies household to household and even kid to kid. A subscription box or a streaming service rarely carries the same weight as a weekly activity a child has built friendships and identity around; cutting the former usually goes unnoticed, while cutting the latter can land hard. Naomi and Theo kept their younger daughter's Saturday soccer team fully intact through their entire gap, while quietly switching from name-brand groceries to store-brand equivalents and pausing a subscription meal kit — changes their kids never mentioned noticing, because nothing about their actual routine had shifted. The goal isn't cutting the cheapest items first; it's cutting the items that matter least to a specific child's sense of normal, which requires knowing your own kids well enough to make that call thoughtfully rather than mechanically.

What to actually say, by rough age range

Children benefit from honest, age-calibrated information rather than either full detail or a vague reassurance that turns out not to match what they're picking up on anyway. For younger children, roughly under eight, a short, concrete, reassuring statement tends to work best: a parent's job ended, the family is figuring out the plan together, and specific routines they care about — naming them directly — aren't changing. For school-age children, a bit more explanation is usually appropriate:

acknowledging that the family is being more careful with spending for a while, framing it as a temporary, manageable situation rather than a crisis, and inviting questions rather than delivering a single scripted announcement. For teenagers, more direct honesty generally serves the relationship better than a softened version they're likely to see through anyway, including, where appropriate, being honest about the general timeline uncertainty covered in Chapter Three, since most teenagers can handle uncertainty better than they can handle a sense of being managed or kept in the dark.

Watching for a kid who's absorbing more than they're saying

Some children process stress by voicing questions directly; others go quiet, or channel the anxiety into an unrelated area — sleep, schoolwork, a younger sibling relationship — without ever naming money as the cause. It's worth watching, gently, for signs that a child is carrying more of this than their behavior around the topic directly suggests, and creating low-pressure openings for them to ask what they're actually wondering about, rather than assuming silence means untroubled. Imani noticed her older child had started asking unusually specific questions about whether they'd have to move, despite no housing conversation ever having happened where he could have overheard it — a sign, once she asked directly, that he'd pieced together fragments from adult conversations and filled the gaps with a worse story than reality, precisely the pattern Chapter One warned against for adults and which applies just as much to children left to guess.

Letting kids help, in small, appropriately sized ways

For school-age children and teenagers in particular, being given a small, genuine way to contribute — packing a lunch instead of buying one, taking on a small chore that used to be paid for externally, being consulted on a minor discretionary decision — can shift a child's experience from passive worry to active, appropriately scaled participation, which many kids find genuinely stabilizing rather than burdensome, provided the ask stays proportional to their age and isn't secretly asking them to carry adult-sized weight.

When kids offer to help in ways that overshoot

Occasionally a child, especially an older one who's picked up on the seriousness of the situation, offers something disproportionate to their age — a teenager suggesting they drop an activity that actually matters to them, or offering to take on a part-time job at the expense of schoolwork that matters more to their longer-term prospects than the modest income would matter to the household's gap. These offers usually come from a genuine, generous place, and they deserve a warm, appreciative response rather than a dismissive one — paired with a clear, honest redirection: thanking them for the offer, and being specific about why the household isn't taking them up on it, so the teenager understands their concern was heard rather than simply brushed aside. The goal, covered earlier in this chapter, is appropriately scaled participation, not a child quietly absorbing adult-sized responsibility because no one redirected the offer clearly.

Grandparents and other extended family in the routine

If grandparents or other extended family play a regular role in a child's routine — school pickup, weekend visits, an ongoing activity together — it's worth including them, at an appropriate level of detail, in the same honest disclosure this chapter recommends for the child directly, since they're often present for exactly the small moments a child might mention something to that a parent never hears about firsthand. A brief, direct conversation lets them reinforce the same calm, consistent message the household has agreed on, rather than improvising their own version if a child asks them a question a parent hasn't prepared them for.

This Week's Crossing

- Identify the one or two routines that matter most to each child in your household, and protect those specifically, even while cutting elsewhere.
- Have an age-calibrated conversation with each child, matched to what they can actually process, rather than a single script delivered to everyone at once.
- Watch for signs a child is absorbing more anxiety than they're voicing directly, and create a low-pressure opening for questions this week.

Chapter 10: Should We Use Savings?

Almost every household facing an income gap arrives, sooner or later, at the same uncomfortable question: should we start drawing down savings now, or hold off as long as possible? Neither instinct — spend savings freely from day one, or refuse to touch them under almost any circumstance — turns out to be reliably right, because the correct answer depends on a deliberate order of operations rather than a single rule, and getting that order right protects a household considerably better than either extreme.

Why "never touch savings" isn't automatically the safest instinct

Some households, particularly ones who worked hard to build a reserve in the first place, treat that reserve as something close to untouchable, cutting every other cost aggressively before drawing on it at all. This instinct comes from a reasonable place, but it can produce a worse outcome than a more deliberate order would, particularly if it means carrying high-interest debt while a low-interest or interest-free reserve sits unused. Savings exist, in this specific situation, precisely to be used for something like this — the discomfort of watching a reserve shrink is real, but it's a different, more manageable kind of discomfort than the compounding cost of high-interest debt accumulating in parallel while savings are protected out of an instinct that made more sense in ordinary times.

A workable order of operations

A useful default sequence, adjustable to a specific household's situation, runs roughly as follows. First, exhaust genuinely free or low-cost options before touching savings at all — this includes the renegotiated terms from Chapter Six, confirmed income support from Chapter Seven, and any truly discretionary cuts identified in the bill inventory from Chapter Five. Second, once those options are exhausted, cover essential costs — housing, minimum debt payments, insurance, utilities — from savings before touching anything else, since these are the costs whose disruption carries the most serious downstream consequences. Third, treat any remaining discretionary spending as the last category to draw from savings for, and the first category to cut further if the gap runs longer than expected. This order isn't a rigid formula — a household's specific debt interest rates, for instance, might reasonably move some debt payments earlier in the sequence, particularly high-interest debt that compounds faster than the discomfort of watching savings shrink justifies avoiding.

Setting a floor before you start spending down

One decision worth making deliberately, before any savings are actually spent, is where the floor sits — the minimum balance the household won't go below without a much larger conversation, distinct from ordinary spending-down decisions. This floor doesn't need to be large; even a modest, explicitly agreed number gives a household an early warning system rather than discovering the account is nearly empty only when it actually is. Wendell and his household set a floor at a level equal to roughly three weeks of committed costs, agreeing explicitly that reaching that floor would trigger an immediate, unscheduled Bridge Reading rather than waiting for the next regular one — a small structural decision that turned a potential moment of panic, months later when they did briefly approach that floor, into a calm, already-planned-for conversation instead.

What "using savings" doesn't have to mean

It's worth separating two things that often get conflated: drawing down a savings account, and abandoning every financial goal that account was originally meant to support. Using reserve funds during a genuine, unchosen income gap isn't a failure of the plan those funds were built for — protecting a household through exactly this kind of disruption is very often what that reserve was for in the first place, even if the household didn't consciously frame it that way when building it. Tobias had built a modest reserve over several years specifically as a general safety net, without a defined purpose beyond "something might come up," and found real relief once he reframed drawing on it during his client's contract loss not as derailing a plan, but as that exact plan working as intended.

Retirement accounts and other savings with real strings attached

Certain kinds of savings — retirement accounts in particular, and some other tax-advantaged or restricted accounts — carry real costs to accessing them early: penalties, tax consequences, or a permanent reduction in long-term growth that a general savings account doesn't carry. These deserve a genuinely separate conversation from ordinary savings, ideally with a clear-eyed look at the actual penalty or cost involved rather than either an automatic "never" or an automatic "it's fine, I'll deal with it later." If a household's situation seems to be heading toward needing to consider this category, it's worth a direct conversation with a qualified financial or tax professional familiar with the household's specific accounts and jurisdiction, rather than working from a general rule of thumb in a book like this one.

The emotional weight of watching a number shrink

Even a well-reasoned, correctly sequenced decision to draw down savings can carry real emotional weight that a pure calculation doesn't account for — a reserve built over years, watched shrinking week by week, can produce a kind of grief that's worth acknowledging rather than dismissing as irrational simply because the underlying financial logic is sound. It can help to reframe what's actually happening: the money isn't disappearing without purpose, it's doing precisely the job it was set aside to do, converting into housing stability, food, and coverage during a period when the household's income couldn't provide those things on its own. That reframe doesn't erase the discomfort, but it tends to make it easier to sit with, which matters over a gap that may run for months rather than days.

Joint accounts, separate accounts, and who watches the number

For partnered households with separate accounts alongside any joint ones, it's worth deciding explicitly whose savings get drawn down first, and in what proportion, rather than leaving that decision to whoever happens to check their balance first during a tight week. This doesn't need to be a rigid, permanently fixed formula — it needs to be a decision made together, during a Bridge Reading, rather than one partner discovering after the fact that their individual reserve carried more of the household's weight than they'd realized or agreed to.

Revisiting the order as circumstances change

The order of operations in this chapter isn't a decision made once and locked in for the duration of a gap — it's worth revisiting at each Bridge Reading, particularly if the gap runs longer than expected, since a sequence that made sense in week two can reasonably shift by week ten as new information about the timeline, new income sources, or new costs enter the picture. Treating this as a living decision, checked regularly alongside the household's other numbers, tends to produce better outcomes than treating it as a single choice made under the pressure of the first difficult week and never revisited again.

This Week's Crossing

- Confirm your household has exhausted the free and low-cost options — renegotiation, income support, discretionary cuts — before drawing further on savings.
- Set an explicit floor balance that, if reached, triggers an immediate unscheduled Bridge Reading rather than waiting for the next regular check.
- If your situation might involve tapping a retirement account or other restricted savings, treat that specifically as a conversation for a qualified professional rather than a decision to make alone from general guidance.

Chapter 11: Side Income Without the Panic Hustle

There's a particular version of "doing something about it" that shows up often during an income gap, and it deserves a closer look before committing real time to it: the sudden, all-consuming pursuit of side income, often across several unrelated efforts at once, driven less by a clear financial calculation than by an urgent need to feel like something productive is happening. This instinct is understandable — bridge income, chosen well, is a genuinely useful piece of Load-bearing work covered in this chapter — but pursued without a clear filter, it tends to produce exhaustion without matching financial benefit, which leaves a household worse positioned, not better, to handle a gap that may still have real distance left to cross.

The difference between bridge income and a panic hustle

Bridge income, done well, is deliberately narrow: one or two manageable options, chosen for their specific fit with a household's actual skills, available time, and realistic earning potential, pursued with a clear sense of how much they're expected to contribute. A panic hustle, by contrast, tends to be broad and reactive — signing up for several unrelated gig platforms in the same week, chasing whichever opportunity was most recently mentioned by a friend or an online forum, measuring effort rather than actual return. The distinguishing question is simple, even if answering it honestly takes real self-awareness: is this specific option worth pursuing because it's likely to produce a meaningful, calculable contribution to the household's runway, or because pursuing it makes the anxiety of sitting still feel more bearable for an afternoon.

Matching the option to the actual time available

The single most common mismatch in this category is time: a bridge-income option chosen without a clear sense of how many hours a household genuinely has available, particularly a household still managing a job search, childcare, or both. Ruth considered, briefly, a fairly involved freelance consulting arrangement that would have required roughly fifteen hours a week — time she didn't actually have once her job search, which she'd correctly identified as the higher-priority use of her time during this specific gap, was accounted for honestly. She chose a narrower, lower-commitment option instead — a few hours a week of paid tutoring in a subject she already knew well — that produced a smaller but genuinely sustainable contribution without competing directly with the activity most likely to end the gap altogether.

Calculating whether an option is actually worth it

Before committing meaningful time to any bridge-income option, it's worth running a quick, honest calculation: realistic hourly earnings after accounting for any upfront costs, minus the time that option takes away from higher-priority activities like a job search or the essential household functioning covered in Chapter Nine, equals the option's real net value to the household. Some options that sound appealing on the surface — a resale side business requiring meaningful upfront inventory investment, a gig requiring an expensive equipment purchase before the first dollar is earned — turn out, once calculated honestly, to carry more risk and slower payback than a simpler, lower-glamour option that starts producing income the same week. This calculation doesn't need to be elaborate. It needs to happen before committing real time or money, rather than after.

Protecting the job search, if there is one

For households where a job search is actively underway, it's worth treating that search itself as the highest-priority use of available time in most cases, and evaluating any bridge-income option specifically against how much it competes with search time rather than in isolation. A bridge-income option that pays modestly but leaves search time genuinely protected is usually a better fit than a higher-paying option that consumes most of the hours that would otherwise go toward the activity most likely to close the gap for good. This isn't a universal rule — a household in a longer, more established gap covered in Chapter Sixteen may reasonably shift this balance — but it's worth naming as the default starting assumption for most situations early in a gap.

When the honest answer is: not right now

For some households, in some weeks, the honest answer to whether to pursue bridge income at all is no — not because the household doesn't need the money, but because the available time is already fully committed to job searching, childcare, or simply the ordinary functioning of a household under real strain, and adding a bridge-income commitment on top would produce more exhaustion than financial benefit. This is a legitimate answer, not a failure to be resourceful, and revisiting the question at the next Bridge Reading rather than forcing a decision this week is often the more sustainable path.

Watching for offers that target exactly this moment

Households in an income gap are, unfortunately, a known target for a specific category of predatory offer — work-from-home opportunities requiring an upfront fee, investment schemes promising unusually fast returns, or advance-fee arrangements that ask for money before any income materializes. These offers tend to be marketed with language that speaks directly to the anxiety of an income gap, which is precisely what makes them effective and precisely why it's worth naming the warning signs directly: any legitimate opportunity that requires you to pay meaningfully before you earn, that pressures you to decide immediately, or that promises returns noticeably better than anything else available deserves real skepticism rather than the benefit of the doubt a stressful moment might otherwise extend to it. When in doubt, the same two-question filter from earlier in this chapter still applies — run the honest net-value calculation, and be especially suspicious of any option that resists that kind of scrutiny.

Turning an existing skill into income without overcommitting

The most sustainable bridge-income options tend to draw on a skill or interest a person already has, rather than requiring an entirely new one to be learned under pressure — Ruth's tutoring drew directly on decades of professional experience she already possessed, requiring no ramp-up time before it could start producing income. Before considering an option that requires meaningful new training or a steep learning curve, it's worth weighing that time cost honestly against a less glamorous option that could start producing income the same week, since speed to first dollar earned often matters more during a gap than the theoretical ceiling of a more ambitious option.

This Week's Crossing

- Run the honest net-value calculation on any bridge-income option you're considering before committing real time or money to it.
- If a job search is underway, evaluate any bridge-income option specifically against how much search time it consumes, not just how much it pays.
- If the honest answer this week is "not right now," treat that as a legitimate decision, and revisit the question at your next Bridge Reading rather than forcing it.

Chapter 12: Housing: Stay, Downsize, or Share?

Housing is usually a household's single largest fixed cost, which means it's also usually the first place anxious attention turns during an income gap, and the place where the biggest, least reversible decisions live. This chapter treats the housing question specifically as what it is in this book's context — a decision made under a forced, unchosen transition, with a genuinely uncertain timeline — rather than the way housing decisions are usually framed in general personal-finance advice, as a lifestyle choice made with full information and no time pressure.

Why this decision deserves more deliberation than most others

Almost every other decision covered in this book is either reversible or bounded in scale — a renegotiated bill can be renegotiated again, a paused subscription can be reactivated, a bridge-income effort can simply stop. Housing decisions are frequently neither: breaking a lease, selling a home, or moving in with family typically can't be undone quickly or cheaply if the gap turns out shorter than expected, which means this is exactly the category of decision Chapter Three's advice about reversibility applies to most directly. That doesn't mean housing changes are never the right call — for some households, in some situations, they clearly are — it means the bar for making one should be higher than the bar for a bill renegotiation, and the timeline range from Chapter Three deserves a central place in weighing it.

The three questions worth answering before the three options

Before comparing staying, downsizing, or sharing housing as options, it helps to answer three questions honestly, since the right answer for a given household depends heavily on how these land. First: what does the updated Span from Chapter Seven actually show — does the household's mapped runway comfortably cover the shorter end of the timeline range, the longer end, or neither? Second: how much of the household's monthly committed cost, from the inventory in Chapter Five, does housing represent specifically, and how much genuine flexibility exists elsewhere in the budget before housing needs to move? Third: what would the actual cost of change be — moving expenses, a broken lease penalty, the disruption to children's routines covered in Chapter Nine — measured against the monthly savings a change would produce, to see how many months it would take to recoup that cost.

Staying put, deliberately rather than by default

For many households, particularly ones whose runway from Chapter Seven comfortably covers a realistic timeline, staying in place while tightening other categories is the right call, and it's worth reaching that conclusion deliberately rather than simply defaulting to it out of inertia or anxiety about disruption. Naomi and Theo ran this exact calculation in their third week and found that their mortgage, while their largest single cost, represented a smaller share of their total budget than they'd assumed, and that their fourteen-week runway comfortably covered even the longer end of their timeline range without touching housing at all — a conclusion that let them stop worrying about a decision they didn't actually need to make, and redirect that attention toward the bills and subscriptions where real, lower-cost flexibility existed instead.

Downsizing, and what it actually saves once real costs are counted

Downsizing — moving to a smaller or less expensive place — can produce real monthly savings, but the calculation needs to include the full cost of the move itself, not just the difference between old and new rent or mortgage figures. Moving costs, any penalty for breaking an existing lease early, a potential gap between move-out and move-in dates, and the time and energy cost of the move itself all belong in the real comparison. For a household with a genuinely long or fully open-ended timeline, these upfront costs are usually recouped quickly by ongoing monthly savings. For a household whose gap might reasonably close within a couple of months, the math often doesn't favor a move at all, even if the theoretical monthly savings look appealing on paper.

Sharing housing, and why it's worth considering without embarrassment

Temporarily sharing housing — moving in with family, taking in a housemate, or combining households with another family member facing a similar situation — carries a stigma in some households that isn't matched by its actual financial usefulness. Zoe and Malik spent six weeks living with Zoe's sister during the middle of their gap, a decision that initially felt like an admission of failure to both of them and that, in practice, meaningfully extended their runway while their two kids adjusted better than either parent expected, largely because the adults kept the kids' daily routines consistent even as the physical location changed. This option isn't right for every household or every family relationship, but it's worth evaluating on its actual merits rather than ruling it out purely on the basis of how it might look to others — a theme Chapter Fourteen returns to directly.

Renters and homeowners face different levers

The three options in this chapter apply differently depending on whether a household rents or owns. A renting household generally has more flexibility to downsize or relocate quickly, but less room to renegotiate the underlying cost structure the way a homeowner might explore refinancing or a payment deferral with a mortgage lender. A homeowning household typically faces higher costs and more friction to change housing quickly, but has options — a temporary mortgage forbearance or modification, in particular — worth investigating directly with a lender using the same proactive approach from Chapter Six, well before any payment is missed. Neither position is simply better than the other during a gap; each comes with its own specific set of levers worth understanding clearly before deciding what, if anything, to change.

A fourth option worth considering: a temporary sublet or house-swap

Beyond staying, downsizing, and sharing, some households find a temporary sublet of part of their existing space, or a short-term house-swap arrangement with a relative or friend in a lower-cost area, offers a middle path — smaller in scale and easier to reverse than a full move, while still producing meaningful savings or income. This isn't available to every household, depending on lease terms, local regulations, and the specific relationship required to make a swap work, but it's worth a moment's consideration before assuming the only real choices are the three named in this chapter's title.

This Week's Crossing

- Answer the three questions — runway coverage, housing's share of the budget, and the true cost-to-recoup timeline of any change — before comparing specific housing options.
- If staying put is the right call, decide that deliberately and note it in your plan, rather than leaving the question quietly unresolved in the back of your mind.
- If a housing change seems worth considering, calculate the full cost of the move itself before comparing it against the monthly savings it would produce.

Chapter 13: The Coverage Gap

Health coverage and other employment-linked benefits have a way of quietly lapsing during an income gap, precisely because they're easy to overlook in the early, more urgent scramble of confirming income and cutting costs — and a coverage gap that goes unnoticed tends to surface at the worst possible moment, when it's needed and no longer there, rather than at a moment when it could still be addressed calmly. This chapter treats coverage as its own distinct piece of Load, deserving direct attention rather than an assumption that it'll sort itself out along with everything else.

Why coverage deserves its own chapter, not just a line in the inventory

Coverage is different from most other bills in one important way: the cost of a gap in coverage often doesn't show up as a monthly number at all — it shows up, if it shows up, as a single large and unpredictable cost at exactly the moment a household can least absorb it. This asymmetry — small, easy-to-defer effort now, versus potentially large, unpredictable cost later — is exactly the kind of tradeoff that's easy to deprioritize under the pressure of more immediately visible costs like housing and debt payments, which is why it earns a dedicated chapter here rather than staying folded into the general bill inventory from Chapter Five.

Mapping what coverage existed, and when it actually ends

The first task is establishing, precisely, what coverage the household had through the lost employment, and the exact date each piece actually ends — which is sometimes, confusingly, not the same date the employment itself ended, since some coverage continues for a defined period afterward. This requires going back to actual documentation rather than assuming based on memory, since benefit continuation terms vary considerably by employer, by type of coverage, and by jurisdiction. Imani discovered, during this step, that her family's health coverage through Sam's former employer actually continued for a further several weeks beyond his last day of active work — a detail buried in a benefits document neither of them had read closely at the time, and one that meaningfully changed how urgently they needed to arrange alternative coverage.

The options worth investigating, without assuming any single one applies

Depending on jurisdiction and household circumstance, several categories of alternative coverage are worth investigating directly rather than assumed: continuing employer coverage temporarily through a formal continuation program where one exists, coverage through a spouse or partner's own employer if applicable, marketplace or public coverage options available in your region, and, for some households, coverage through a professional association, alumni organization, or similar group that offers plans independent of employment. Because coverage systems vary significantly by country and even by region within a country, this book deliberately doesn't recommend a single specific path — the useful action is investigating what's actually available to your household directly, ideally starting before existing coverage lapses rather than after.

What to do if coverage does lapse before a replacement is in place

If a genuine gap in coverage does open up — a real possibility for some households despite careful planning — it's worth knowing, in advance if possible, what emergency options exist in your area for urgent needs during an uncovered window, and treating any deferrable, non-urgent care as worth postponing briefly if a replacement is confirmed to be close. This isn't a comfortable category to plan for, and it's exactly the kind of planning that's much easier to do calmly in advance than to figure out in the middle of an actual urgent need, which is the core argument for addressing this chapter early rather than letting it wait behind more visible bills.

Coverage for the specific people who need it most

Households with children, with an existing health condition in the family, or with regular prescription needs carry a meaningfully higher stake in closing a coverage gap quickly than a household without those factors, and it's worth being honest about which category your household falls into rather than applying a generic level of urgency to everyone. Wendell, whose household included a family member with regular prescription needs, treated this chapter's work as his single highest priority in the week after his layoff, ahead even of the bill renegotiation covered in Chapter Six, precisely because the cost of a gap here was both larger and less predictable than anything else on his list.

Keeping this on the Bridge Reading, not just handling it once

Like the bill inventory in Chapter Five, coverage status belongs as a recurring line in the household's Bridge Reading rather than a single check performed once and set aside — a temporary coverage arrangement that was correct three weeks ago may need updating as the timeline range from Chapter Three shifts, particularly if a gap runs longer than its shorter estimate suggested it might.

The coverage people forget to check

Health coverage tends to get the most attention during this kind of review, understandably, but it's worth deliberately checking a short list of easily overlooked categories too: dental and vision coverage, which sometimes lapse on a different schedule than primary health coverage; life insurance, particularly any policy that was employer-provided rather than individually owned; and disability coverage, which matters more than most households realize until they need it. None of these carry the same urgency as primary health coverage for most households, but each is worth a specific, deliberate check rather than an assumption that "coverage" as a single category has already been fully addressed once the main health plan question is settled.

When replacement coverage costs more than expected

Sometimes the alternative coverage options a household investigates turn out to be more expensive than the coverage lost, which can feel like an unfair extra burden layered on top of an already difficult situation. When this happens, it's worth treating the replacement premium itself as a line in the bill inventory from Chapter Five, sorted honestly by its actual flexibility — some coverage genuinely has lower-cost tiers worth exploring, while other coverage, particularly for a household with real medical needs, may simply need to be treated as a fixed, essential cost even at a higher price than hoped, weighed against the far larger and less predictable cost of going without it.

A brief note on prescription costs specifically

For households managing an ongoing prescription, it's worth asking a pharmacist directly, during this same week, about generic alternatives, manufacturer assistance programs, or a shorter-term bridge supply if a coverage transition is still in progress — pharmacists are frequently the fastest, most direct source of practical options in this specific category, more so than a general search, and most are glad to help a household navigate a temporary coverage gap around a medication that matters.

This Week's Crossing

- Confirm the exact date every piece of employment-linked coverage actually ends, using real documentation rather than memory.
- Investigate the specific alternative coverage options available in your region, starting before any existing coverage lapses if at all possible.
- If your household includes anyone with regular medical or prescription needs, treat closing this gap as a top priority this week, ahead of less urgent items on your list.

Chapter 14: Tell Your Network What's True

Most people, in the first weeks after an income loss, either say almost nothing to anyone outside their immediate household, or say something vague enough that it doesn't actually invite the kind of help that a more honest version might. Both instincts come from an understandable place — a wish to avoid pity, a fear of being seen differently, a hope that the situation resolves quickly enough that wider disclosure never becomes necessary — and both instincts, held too tightly for too long, tend to cut a household off from exactly the kind of practical support a wider network is often genuinely willing to offer, if only it knew what was actually happening.

Why vague disclosure tends to help less than honest disclosure

There's a specific pattern worth noticing: a vague update like "things have been a bit hectic lately" or "we're going through some changes" satisfies a wish to say something without saying too much, but it doesn't give anyone in your network the specific information they'd need to actually help — a job lead relevant to your field, a connection to someone hiring, an invitation to something that would otherwise have cost money. Honest, bounded disclosure — true, specific, and appropriately limited in detail — tends to produce meaningfully more useful support than either silence or vagueness, precisely because it gives people something concrete to act on rather than something to simply feel sympathetic about.

What "bounded" means, and why it matters

Honest disclosure doesn't mean total disclosure. There's a real and useful middle ground between saying nothing and sharing every financial detail of your household's situation, and finding that middle ground is what makes this kind of honesty sustainable rather than exposing. A workable version might sound like: "Theo's position was eliminated last month when his company closed its regional office. He's actively looking for something in logistics or operations management, and if you hear of anything, I'd genuinely appreciate you passing it along." This tells the truth, gives specific, actionable information, and stops well short of disclosing account balances, specific numbers, or details that belong only inside the household's own Bridge Reading conversations.

Choosing who to tell, and in what order

Not every relationship needs the same disclosure at the same time, and it's reasonable to sequence this deliberately rather than announcing the situation to everyone at once. Close family and close friends, who are likely to offer genuine support and unlikely to judge, are usually worth telling early and more fully. A wider professional network — former colleagues, industry contacts, people specifically positioned to help with a job search — is worth telling specifically and with a clear ask, even if the relationship is less personally close, precisely because these are often the connections most likely to produce an actual lead. Wider social circles, extended family, and more casual acquaintances can reasonably come later, and with a somewhat more general version of the same honest, bounded framing.

When network disclosure directly produces results

Ruth's decision to tell a former colleague, three weeks into her search, exactly what had happened and exactly what kind of role she was looking for led directly to an introduction that eventually became her new position five months later — a connection that wouldn't have happened if her early updates to that same colleague had stayed at the vague "just taking some time to figure out next steps" level she'd initially defaulted to out of a habit of not wanting to seem like she was asking for anything. This isn't a guarantee that disclosure produces a job lead every time, but it consistently produces more opportunities for one than silence does, simply by giving more people accurate information to act on.

Handling the reactions that don't help

Not every response to honest disclosure will be useful, and it's worth being prepared for a small number of unhelpful reactions — unsolicited financial advice, a comparison to someone else's very different situation, a question that feels more curious than caring — without letting a handful of these responses become a reason to retreat back into silence with everyone else. A short, neutral response — "we're managing it, but I appreciate you asking" — closes down an unhelpful thread without requiring a longer explanation, and doesn't need to change how openly you tell the next person, whose reaction may well be more useful.

Disclosure as part of the crossing, not a separate task

This chapter's work sits squarely under the Crossing category from Chapter Four, alongside the partner conversations from Chapter Eight and the family conversations from Chapter Nine — all three are, at their core, about making sure the people around you have accurate information rather than filling a gap with guesses, and about letting a wider circle of people actually help, rather than carrying the entire crossing alone out of a wish to appear unaffected.

A brief word on social media specifically

Social platforms deserve their own quick mention, since they sit somewhere between close disclosure and wide disclosure and don't always behave the way either category would predict. A public post announcing a job search can occasionally produce a genuine, useful lead from an unexpected corner of your network, but it also broadcasts the situation to a far wider and less curated audience than a direct conversation does, including people whose reactions you have far less ability to predict or manage. Many households find a middle path works best: a more private, direct message to specific, relevant contacts, reserving any public post for a later stage, once the initial disorientation has settled and a specific, well-worded ask has been thought through deliberately rather than posted in the heat of the first difficult week.

Professional associations and alumni networks

Beyond personal and social contacts, it's worth deliberately reaching out to any professional association, industry group, or educational alumni network you belong to, even loosely — these organizations often maintain job boards, mentorship programs, or member directories specifically designed for exactly this kind of disclosure and request, and they tend to carry less of the social awkwardness some people feel disclosing to personal contacts, since sharing a job search through a professional channel is precisely what those channels exist for.

What honest disclosure sounds like from the other side

It can help, before making these calls or having these conversations, to remember what it feels like to be on the receiving end of one — most people, told honestly and specifically what a friend or colleague needs, feel trusted and glad to have been asked, not burdened. Naomi found this out directly when a colleague she'd hesitated to tell responded not with pity but with a genuine, practical lead within the same week — a reminder that the anticipation of disclosure is very often heavier than the actual conversation turns out to be.

This Week's Crossing

- Draft one honest, bounded version of your situation — true, specific, appropriately limited — that you'd feel comfortable saying to a close contact this week.
- Identify three people in your wider network specifically positioned to help, and reach out to them with a clear, honest update and a specific ask.
- Prepare a short, neutral response for an unhelpful reaction, so one awkward conversation doesn't talk you out of being honest with the next person.

Chapter 15: The Monthly Bridge Reading

Every practice covered so far in this book eventually needs to settle into a sustainable rhythm, or it drifts — the bill inventory goes stale, the timeline range stops getting updated, the partner check-ins happen only when something's already gone wrong rather than on a predictable schedule. The Bridge Reading, introduced briefly in Chapter Four, is this book's answer to that drift, and this chapter builds it out fully: what it actually involves, how it evolves as a gap continues, and how a household knows it's time to shift from a weekly rhythm to a monthly one.

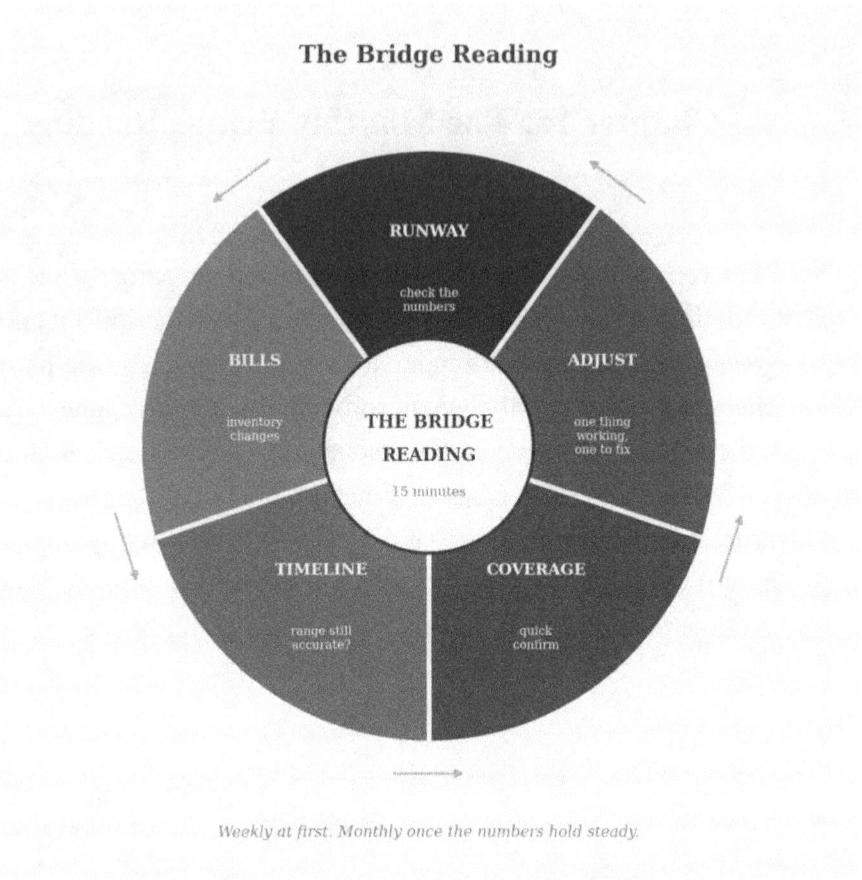

The Bridge Reading: five checkpoints, fifteen minutes, on a fixed rhythm.

From weekly to monthly: recognizing the shift

The earliest weeks of an income gap are usually the most volatile — new information arriving constantly, decisions still being made across nearly every chapter of this book at once, a level of change that really benefits from a weekly check-in rather than a monthly one. That volatility typically settles, for most households, somewhere in the four-to-six-week range, though this varies considerably and isn't a deadline to hit on schedule. The signal worth watching for isn't a calendar date — it's whether a given week's Bridge Reading is mostly confirming that nothing significant has changed, rather than surfacing new decisions that need to be made. Once two or three consecutive weekly readings look like that, it's usually time to shift to a monthly rhythm, which most households find considerably easier to sustain over a longer gap without it becoming a source of fatigue in its own right.

What belongs in every reading, regardless of rhythm

A useful Bridge Reading, whether weekly or monthly, walks through the same short list of checkpoints each time, ideally in the same order, so the whole thing takes fifteen minutes rather than becoming its own dreaded task. Check the triage and runway numbers from Chapter Two against where they stood at the last reading. Check the bill inventory from Chapter Five for any changes — a newly negotiated rate, a subscription that needs cancelling, a bill that's shifted. Check the timeline range from Chapter Three against any new information, and adjust it if the picture has actually changed. Check coverage status from Chapter Thirteen briefly, even when nothing's expected to have changed, simply to confirm it hasn't. Note one thing that's working and one thing that needs a small adjustment before the next reading. That's the entire structure — five short checks, not a full rebuild of the household's finances each time.

Keeping it fifteen minutes, on purpose

The discipline of keeping a Bridge Reading truly short is more important than it might seem, because a check-in that regularly runs long or turns into an extended, difficult conversation is a check-in households start avoiding, which defeats its entire purpose. If a specific issue surfaces during a reading that clearly needs more discussion than fifteen minutes allows — a bigger decision about housing, a harder conversation about a partner's job search timeline — the right move is naming that issue, scheduling a separate, dedicated conversation for it, and letting the Bridge Reading itself stay short and sustainable. Zoe and Malik learned this by trial early on, after their first few readings kept expanding into hour-long conversations that left both of them avoiding the next one; splitting out bigger topics into their own separate conversations, while keeping the core reading itself strictly to its five checkpoints, made the practice sustainable again almost immediately.

Doing it even when there's nothing new to report

There's a temptation, once a gap has settled into a stable rhythm with little changing week to week, to skip a reading that feels like it won't surface anything new. This is usually a mistake, and not because the reading itself will necessarily reveal something — most of the time, in a stable stretch, it won't — but because the discipline of the recurring check is what keeps a household from drifting out of shared accuracy without noticing. A skipped reading rarely causes a problem on its own; a pattern of skipped readings is usually how a household ends up caught off guard, weeks later, by a number or a coverage gap that a regular check would have caught early and quietly.

When the reading itself becomes the good news

For most households, the Bridge Reading eventually becomes less a source of anxiety and more a small, reassuring ritual — a fixed point in the week or month where a household confirms, together, that the plan is still holding, the numbers are still accounted for, and nothing has quietly slipped through unnoticed.

That shift, from dread to routine reassurance, is itself a meaningful sign that a household has moved from the acute early stage of an income gap into a more sustainable, manageable stretch — exactly the transition Part Four addresses next, for the households whose bridge turns out to run longer than they initially hoped.

Choosing a format that will actually get used

The specific format a household uses for its Bridge Reading matters less than whether it's a format the household will actually return to consistently — a simple notebook kept in a kitchen drawer, a shared note on a phone, a basic spreadsheet, or the worksheet template provided in this book's appendix all work equally well as long as the household picks one and sticks with it rather than recreating the format from scratch each time. The households that sustain this practice longest tend to be the ones who made the format nearly frictionless to open and update, rather than the ones who built the most elaborate system in the first week and then found it too cumbersome to maintain by the third or fourth reading.

What a reading looks like when the news is good

Not every Bridge Reading delivers a flat or difficult update, and it's worth deliberately pausing to acknowledge it when one doesn't — a renegotiation that came through better than expected, a runway that's stretched further than the last calculation suggested, a bridge-income effort that's producing more than anticipated. Treating good news within the reading with the same deliberate attention as a problem, rather than rushing past it to the next checkpoint, reinforces the practice as an honestly balanced check on reality rather than a ritual that only ever surfaces things to worry about.

This Week's Crossing

- Decide, honestly, whether your household is still in weekly territory or ready to shift to monthly readings, based on how much is actually still changing week to week.
- Run through the five-checkpoint structure this week, timing yourself to confirm it can genuinely fit inside fifteen minutes.
- If a bigger issue surfaces during the reading, schedule it as its own separate conversation rather than letting it expand the reading itself.

PART FOUR: WHEN THE BRIDGE STRAINS

Chapter 16: When the Bridge Runs Longer Than Planned

Most of this book, so far, has assumed a gap that resolves somewhere within the timeline range built in Chapter Three — uncomfortable, but bounded, with an end that arrives before the household's plan is truly tested. Some gaps run longer than that range, sometimes considerably longer, and this chapter is for the household living through that specific, harder stretch: past the point where "temporary" still feels like an accurate word, without yet having reached the relief of Part Five's return to two incomes.

Naming the shift honestly, without catastrophizing it

There's a specific moment worth naming directly when a gap runs past even the longer end of a household's original timeline range: the temptation either to pretend nothing has changed, or to swing hard into treating the situation as a permanent, life-altering crisis rather than what it actually is — a bridge that's turning out to need a longer span than originally engineered, which calls for reinforcement, not a total redesign. Ruth's gap ran to five months against an original range that topped out around eight weeks, and she found real value in this exact distinction partway through: adjusting her plan to fit the longer reality without concluding, incorrectly, that her situation had become permanent or that everything she'd built so far no longer applied.

Extending the Span without starting over

The practical task, once a gap clearly runs past its original range, is extending the Span rather than discarding the plan built around it. This means returning to Chapter Seven's runway mapping with updated, more conservative figures, returning to Chapter Five's bill inventory to look for additional flexibility that felt unnecessary to pursue when the gap looked shorter, and returning to Chapter Ten's savings order to reassess whether the sequence still holds given a longer expected timeline. None of the underlying method changes. What changes is the specific numbers being plugged into it, and possibly the urgency of certain decisions — bridge income from Chapter Eleven, for instance, often deserves a second look at this stage, even for a household that reasonably deprioritized it early on.

Guarding against decision fatigue

A longer gap brings a specific risk that a shorter one mostly avoids: decision fatigue, the gradual erosion of a household's ability to keep making careful, deliberate choices after weeks or months of doing exactly that. This tends to show up as either increasingly careless spending, driven by simple exhaustion with vigilance, or the opposite, an increasingly rigid, anxious over-monitoring of every purchase that leaves no room for ordinary life to continue. The Bridge Reading rhythm from Chapter Fifteen becomes especially valuable here, precisely because it contains the vigilance to a bounded, predictable window rather than letting it spread across every day, which is a meaningfully sustainable posture for a gap measured in months rather than weeks.

Protecting morale as a genuine budget line

For a longer gap specifically, it's worth treating a small amount of genuinely enjoyable, non-essential spending as a real line item rather than an indulgence to feel guilty about, provided it fits within the household's honestly assessed runway. A modest, deliberately budgeted allowance for something that restores morale — a family outing, a small treat, an evening that has nothing to do with the situation at all — isn't in tension with the discipline this book asks for elsewhere; a household that maintains zero morale spending across a five-month gap is more likely to burn out on the whole method than one that budgets carefully for a small amount of relief along the way. This is Load-bearing work as much as any bill, even though it doesn't look like it on a spreadsheet.

Revisiting bigger decisions that were correctly deferred earlier

Some decisions this book earlier recommended holding off on — a housing change from Chapter Twelve, in particular — deserve a genuine second look once a gap clearly runs long, since the calculation in that chapter depended directly on the timeline range, and a longer confirmed timeline can change which option actually makes financial sense. This isn't a failure of the original decision to stay put; it was correct given the information available at the time. Revisiting it with updated information, at the appropriate point in a longer gap, is simply the method working as intended, not a sign that an earlier choice was wrong.

Knowing this stretch has an end, even without a date

The hardest part of an extended gap is rarely any single decision covered elsewhere in this book — it's the sustained uncertainty itself, month after month, without a firm date to count down to. There's no method in this book, or anywhere else, that removes that uncertainty entirely. What the Bridge Method offers instead is a structure sturdy enough to keep carrying real weight for as long as this specific stretch requires, checked regularly, adjusted as needed, built for a gap rather than for good — which is, in the end, exactly the point of building a bridge instead of a blueprint in the first place.

Recognizing your own version of "long"

What counts as a longer-than-planned gap is relative to each household's own original range from Chapter Three, not a fixed universal number — a household whose range topped out at three weeks experiences week six very differently than a household whose range topped out at four months does. The point of this chapter isn't a specific threshold to watch for; it's the shift in posture once a household's own honest assessment concludes the gap has genuinely outrun its original estimate, whatever that estimate happened to be. Trusting your own numbers over a generic benchmark, here as throughout this book, tends to produce a more accurate and more useful read on where you actually stand.

Reconnecting with your network again, specifically

Chapter Fourteen's disclosure work doesn't end after the first round of conversations, and a longer gap benefits from a second, deliberate wave of outreach to the same network, framed honestly around the situation's continuation rather than treated as awkward to repeat. "Still looking, and still glad to hear about anything that might fit" is a perfectly reasonable follow-up message months after the first one, and it's considerably more effective at surfacing new leads than assuming your network still has the original conversation fresh in mind and will proactively think of you without a reminder.

This Week's Crossing

- If your gap has run past its original timeline range, update your Span, bill inventory, and savings order with current, more conservative figures rather than discarding the plan entirely.
- Budget a small, deliberate amount for morale-restoring spending, sized to fit your actual runway, rather than treating all non-essential spending as off-limits indefinitely.
- Revisit any bigger decision — particularly housing — that was correctly deferred earlier, now that you have a clearer sense of the gap's real length.

Chapter 17: When One Partner Wants to Panic and the Other Wants to Freeze

Chapter Eight covered the ordinary, expected differences between partners facing the same income gap — different fears, different instincts about spending, different preferences for how often to talk about it. For some households, that gap between partners runs deeper than a scheduling fix or a foundational conversation can fully resolve, settling into a genuine, recurring pattern where one partner consistently pushes toward more urgent action and the other consistently pulls toward less, each one increasingly frustrated with what looks, from the outside, like the other person's overreaction or the other person's denial. This chapter is for that deeper pattern specifically.

Recognizing the pattern for what it is

What looks, in the moment, like one partner being reckless and the other being paralyzed is more accurately, in most cases, two different nervous systems responding to the same genuine stress in two different, equally understandable directions — one toward heightened activity and control-seeking, the other toward a kind of protective shutdown. Naming this as a pattern, rather than as a character flaw belonging to one partner, tends to lower the temperature of the disagreement considerably, because it reframes the conflict from "you're wrong about this" to "we respond differently under this kind of pressure, and we need a structure that works for both responses rather than asking one of us to simply become the other."

Why matching the response to the actual math matters more than matching each other

A useful anchor, when this pattern is running hot, is returning to the actual numbers from the household's Bridge Reading rather than litigating the disagreement in the abstract. If the runway from Chapter Seven genuinely supports a calmer pace, the partner pushing toward urgent, aggressive cuts benefits from seeing that concretely, in the actual numbers, rather than being told to simply relax. If the runway genuinely doesn't support the pace the calmer partner has settled into, that partner benefits from seeing that concretely too. The numbers won't resolve every disagreement, but they replace a fight about who's right in general with a narrower, more answerable question about what the actual situation calls for — which is considerably easier to resolve together.

Giving each response style a legitimate role

Rather than treating one partner's instinct as correct and the other's as something to be managed or overridden, it's often more productive to find a legitimate role for each. The partner inclined toward urgent action might reasonably take the lead on the renegotiation calls from Chapter Six or the bridge-income research from Chapter Eleven — tasks that benefit from that energy. The partner inclined toward protective stability might reasonably take the lead on the children's routines from Chapter Nine or the household's day-to-day steadiness — work that benefits from that instinct. This isn't a perfect division for every household, and it isn't about permanently assigning roles, but it converts what feels like a conflict between two responses into a genuine division of labor that uses both.

When the pattern needs more than this book can offer

For some households, this dynamic sits on top of a longer-standing relationship pattern that predates the income gap entirely, and the gap has simply brought it into sharper focus rather than created it from nothing. If the disagreement consistently escalates beyond what a Bridge Reading or a dedicated conversation can resolve, or if it's affecting the relationship in ways that feel bigger than this specific financial situation, that's a reasonable and common enough experience to be worth raising with a couples counselor or a similar qualified professional — not a sign that the household has failed at the method in this book, but a recognition that some patterns benefit from support this book isn't positioned to provide.

What it looks like when both responses are actually useful

Corinne and Dev, whose differing fears surfaced early in their gap in Chapter Eight, found over time that their different instincts genuinely complemented each other once they stopped fighting over which one was correct: Dev's push toward concrete financial action kept their numbers current and their bills renegotiated promptly, while Corinne's instinct toward protecting normalcy kept their household's day-to-day life — including for her aging mother, who lived nearby and noticed more than either of them initially realized — steady and reassuring throughout. Neither instinct, on its own, would have served their household as well as both did together, once each was given a legitimate place in the plan rather than treated as something to overcome.

What kids notice when partners disagree about money

When this particular pattern runs hot in a household with children present, it's worth remembering Chapter Nine's core point: kids register tone and tension far more than content, and a recurring, unresolved disagreement about pace and risk between partners tends to register with children as generalized household anxiety, even when the specific content of the disagreement is never discussed in front of them directly. This isn't a reason to hide every disagreement artificially — that's neither realistic nor healthy — but it is a reason to make sure at least some of this pattern's resolution happens through the structured channels this chapter describes, Bridge Readings and dedicated conversations, rather than through repeated tense exchanges that happen to occur within earshot of a child who's absorbing more of the emotional weather than either parent may realize.

A short exercise for naming the pattern together

A useful, low-stakes way to start this conversation is for each partner to finish the same sentence separately, then compare answers out loud: "When I feel like our money situation is out of control, what I actually want to do is ___." One partner's honest answer might be "make a decision, any decision, right now." The other's might be "stop talking about it for a day so I can think clearly." Neither answer is a criticism of the other person once it's out in the open — it's simply useful, specific information about how each of you is actually wired under this kind of pressure, which tends to be far more productive than arguing about the specific spending decision that happened to trigger the disagreement that day.

Remembering this is a pattern, not a verdict on the relationship

It's worth closing this chapter with a reassurance worth holding onto: a household that recognizes this pattern in itself hasn't discovered a flaw in the relationship, it's discovered ordinary human variation under genuine stress, which nearly every household carrying two adults through a real income gap encounters in some form. Naming it, structuring around it, and giving each response a legitimate role is the method working as intended, not a sign that anything about the partnership itself needs to change.

This Week's Crossing

- Name the pattern directly with your partner, as a difference in stress response rather than a character judgment about either of you.
- Bring your actual Bridge Reading numbers into the next disagreement about pace, and use them to answer the narrower question of what the situation calls for.
- Assign each partner's natural instinct a legitimate, specific role in the plan, rather than asking either of you to override how you actually respond under this kind of pressure.

Chapter 18: The Single-Income Household by Design vs. by Circumstance

Somewhere in the middle of most income gaps, a household runs into a specific, disorienting kind of advice mismatch: a genuinely useful-sounding book, article, or friend's suggestion about "how we live well on one income," aimed at households who chose that arrangement deliberately, with time to plan for it, often for reasons like raising young children or simplifying a lifestyle. That advice frequently doesn't translate well to a household in an unchosen, uncertain-length gap, and this chapter exists to draw that distinction clearly, so it's easier to recognize which advice actually fits your situation and which doesn't, however well-intentioned it is.

Why the two situations look similar but aren't

On the surface, a deliberately chosen single-income household and a household in an unchosen income gap face a similar arithmetic problem — less household income to work with than before. Underneath that surface similarity, the situations differ in ways that matter considerably for which advice applies. A chosen single-income household typically has time to plan the transition in advance, a known and often permanent timeline, and the decision itself carries a very different emotional weight than an unchosen loss does. A household in an unchosen gap is working with an uncertain, probably temporary timeline, decisions made under real time pressure, and an emotional starting point shaped by loss rather than by choice. Advice built for the first situation — restructure your entire budget around permanent single-income living, make major lifestyle changes now that you'll keep long-term — often doesn't fit the second situation well, precisely because it assumes permanence and planning time that an unchosen gap doesn't offer.

Where the advice genuinely does transfer

Some pieces of single-income-household advice transfer well regardless of which situation you're in, and it's worth being able to tell the difference rather than dismissing everything from that category. Practical tactics — meal planning that reduces grocery costs, strategies for finding lower-cost versions of recurring expenses, general principles about needs versus wants — tend to work reasonably well in either situation, since they don't depend on the timeline being permanent. What doesn't transfer well is the larger-scale, irreversible restructuring: selling a second car permanently, making a major and hard-to-reverse housing change, or abandoning a career path entirely, on the assumption that the current arrangement is the new normal, when the household's actual situation is a bridge rather than a blueprint.

A quick filter for evaluating this kind of advice

When encountering a specific piece of advice from this broader category, a useful filter is asking whether it assumes permanence, and if so, whether that assumption actually matches your household's situation. Advice that works equally well whether your gap lasts six weeks or six months is safe to adopt. Advice that only makes sense if the arrangement is going to be permanent is worth setting aside, or at minimum holding loosely, until your Span from Chapter Seven and your ongoing Bridge

Readings from Chapter Fifteen give you a clearer sense of whether "permanent" is actually where things are heading, which for most households in this book's specific situation, it isn't.

Self-employed and irregular-income variations of the same confusion

A related but distinct version of this mismatch shows up for households whose income loss came through a different path than a traditional layoff — a self-employed person whose client base collapsed, a freelancer whose contracts didn't renew, a small-business owner whose revenue dried up. Tobias, working through his own gap after his primary client ended their contract, found a lot of general small-business or freelance-income advice assumed either a thriving, growing practice or a permanently scaled-back one, with very little written for the specific in-between of "this collapsed suddenly and I don't yet know if or when it recovers." The same filter applies here too: adopt what's genuinely timeline-neutral, hold the rest loosely until the actual shape of the gap becomes clearer.

Staying oriented toward the bridge, not the new normal

The underlying point of this chapter connects directly back to Chapter Four's founding distinction: you are building something engineered for a specific, probably temporary gap, not redesigning your household's permanent shape. Advice, however well-meaning, that quietly assumes the second thing deserves a second look before it gets adopted wholesale — not rejected outright, since some of it genuinely helps, but evaluated specifically against whether it fits the bridge you're actually building.

The inspiration trap

A related mismatch is worth naming on its own: content built to inspire — a video essay on the joys of a simpler life, a social feed built around one family's deliberate, well-funded choice to live on one income — can leave a household in an unchosen gap feeling worse rather than better, not because the content is dishonest, but because it's answering a different emotional question than the one an unchosen gap actually raises. A household that chose this arrangement, with savings built for it in advance and a clear sense of why, is telling a story about intention. A household in the middle of an unchosen gap is living a story about disruption, however well it's being managed. Noticing the difference, and giving yourself permission to feel however you actually feel about your own situation rather than measuring it against a story that was never describing your circumstances in the first place, is worth doing consciously rather than leaving to comparison.

Well-meaning advice from people who haven't been here

A related, closely connected experience is advice from people who've never actually lived through an unchosen income gap themselves, offered with real warmth and no real fit — a relative who built wealth slowly over decades suggesting an investment strategy irrelevant to a household needing cash within weeks, a friend whose single-income household was always the plan suggesting a lifestyle change that assumes a permanence this household doesn't have. The same permanence filter from earlier in this chapter works here too, and it's worth remembering that the advice is usually offered in good faith even when it doesn't fit, which makes a gracious "that's helpful, thank you" a reasonable response even when you have no intention of following it.

Why this distinction is worth making explicit, not just intuitive

It would be simpler if households naturally sorted advice by permanence without needing a dedicated chapter to name the habit explicitly, but in practice, advice absorbed during a stressful, information-heavy stretch tends to get adopted or dismissed based on how persuasively it's delivered rather than how well it actually fits the situation. Making the permanence filter an explicit, repeatable habit — asked out loud, of any new piece of advice, rather than assumed automatically — is what keeps a household's plan matched to its actual circumstances rather than to whichever source happened to be most convincing that week.

This Week's Crossing

- Take one piece of single-income advice you've encountered recently and run it through the permanence filter — does it assume this is temporary, or does it assume this is forever?
- Separate any advice you've been following into "timeline-neutral, keep it" and "assumes permanence, hold it loosely" categories.
- If your income loss came through self-employment or freelance work rather than a traditional layoff, note where general advice has been a poor fit, and trust your own household's actual numbers over generic guidance.

Chapter 19: When There's No Severance At All

Much of this book, particularly Chapter Seven, assumes a household has at least some formal severance, notice pay, or structured income support to map against its timeline. Not every income loss comes with any of that. A short-term contract that simply isn't renewed, a small company that closes without the resources to offer severance, a self-employed person whose main client disappears overnight — all of these can produce an income gap every bit as real as a formal layoff, with none of the same structured cushion. This chapter is for that specific, harder starting position.

Why this situation calls for a faster Footings phase, not a different method

The core method in this book doesn't change for a household without severance — Footings, Span, Load, and Crossing still apply in the same order, and the Bridge Reading rhythm still matters just as much. What changes is the pace: without a severance or notice-pay cushion providing an early buffer, the triage math from Chapter Two and the renegotiation work from Chapter Six carry more immediate urgency, and benefit from happening within days rather than over the first couple of weeks. Tobias, whose client relationship ended with essentially no notice and no severance of any kind, ran his triage numbers the same evening he learned his contract wasn't continuing, rather than waiting the few days that a household with a cushion might reasonably take.

Where the runway actually comes from instead

Without severance to map in Chapter Seven's calendar, a household's runway consists entirely of existing savings, any income-support program the situation qualifies for, and household reserves more broadly — which makes the honest triage number from Chapter Two even more central to every decision that follows. It's worth being particularly thorough here about income-support programs: some are specifically designed for exactly this kind of gap, including certain programs available to workers who've lost self-employment income or short-term contract work, and it's worth confirming eligibility directly rather than assuming a program doesn't apply because the job loss didn't look like a traditional layoff.

The renegotiation conversation, adjusted for a shorter runway

The renegotiation scripts from Chapter Six work the same way regardless of whether severance exists, but the framing benefits from slight adjustment when there's no cushion behind the request. Being specific and direct about the absence of any severance or transition income — rather than a vaguer reference to "a change in employment" — often produces a more immediately responsive conversation with a lender or service provider, since it signals genuine urgency rather than a household simply exploring its options at leisure. This isn't about exaggerating the situation; it's about being precise, since precision here tends to be met with more useful options than a softer version of the same request.

Rebuilding an emergency reserve during, not just after, the gap

For households in this situation with little or no existing reserve, the savings-order question from Chapter Ten looks different: there may be little or nothing to draw down, which means the more urgent early task is stabilizing cash flow through renegotiation, income support, and bridge income from Chapter Eleven, rather than managing a drawdown. It's worth setting a modest, realistic goal — even a very small buffer, building slowly through whatever bridge income the household can sustainably manage — rather than treating "we have no cushion" as a reason not to try to build any margin at all during the gap itself.

The disclosure conversation, without the softer framing severance provides

Tell Your Network What's True, from Chapter Fourteen, applies just as directly here, though the framing may need to be slightly different: a formal layoff with severance is sometimes, unfairly, treated as more socially acceptable to disclose than a contract simply not renewing or a self-employed income collapsing, even though both represent a genuine, unchosen loss of income. It's worth naming this directly and refusing the double standard — an honest, bounded version of the truth serves a household's network-based support just as well in this situation as in a more traditional layoff, and the practical benefits of disclosure covered in Chapter Fourteen apply equally here.

What doesn't change: the shape of the bridge itself

However the gap began, and whatever cushion did or didn't come with it, the underlying goal is identical: get the household safely across a distance of currently uncertain width, using the four pillars of Footings, Span, Load, and Crossing, checked on a regular rhythm, sized to the actual situation rather than to a generic plan. A household without severance is simply starting with a narrower Footings phase and a more urgent early pace — not a fundamentally different task.

Documenting the loss even without formal paperwork

A traditional layoff usually comes with some paper trail — a termination letter, a severance agreement, a formal record an employer generates as a matter of course. A contract that simply isn't renewed, or a self-employed client relationship that ends with a phone call or a brief message, often doesn't produce anything similar, which can leave a household without a clear record of exactly what happened and when. It's worth creating that record yourself, even informally — a dated note describing what occurred, copies of any relevant messages or emails, a simple written timeline — both because some income-support programs require documentation you may otherwise struggle to produce later, and because having a clear, dated account of your own makes the triage and disclosure work throughout this book considerably easier to do with confidence.

A lesson for the next contract, once this gap closes

For a household whose income comes primarily through contract or freelance work, this specific gap is worth treating as a prompt to review future contract terms once things stabilize — specifically, whether future agreements include a defined notice period or termination clause, which can turn a future ending into something closer to the severance-mapping situation in Chapter Seven rather than the abrupt, unpaperworked ending covered in this chapter. This isn't always negotiable, and some clients or platforms won't offer it regardless of what's requested, but it costs nothing to ask for in a future negotiation, and Tobias, once his gap closed, made it a standard request in every new client agreement going forward.

This Week's Crossing

- If your income loss came without severance or notice pay, run your triage numbers from Chapter Two immediately rather than waiting for a calmer moment.
- Confirm eligibility for any income-support program that applies to contract, self-employed, or short-notice job loss specifically, rather than assuming the standard programs don't fit your situation.
- Set a modest, realistic goal for building even a small reserve during the gap itself, rather than treating the absence of an existing cushion as a reason not to try.

Chapter 20: Retirement, Long-Term Goals, and What Not to Sacrifice

Chapter Ten touched briefly on retirement accounts and other restricted savings as a category deserving its own conversation, distinct from ordinary savings, because of the real penalties and long-term costs that can come with tapping them early. This chapter is that fuller conversation — for the household weighing whether a long-term goal needs to be interrupted, reduced, or protected outright during an income gap, and how to think clearly about that decision rather than either an automatic "never touch it" or an automatic "I'll deal with the consequences later."

Why retirement savings deserve a different category of thinking

Ordinary savings and retirement accounts solve genuinely different problems, even though both sit under the broad heading of "money set aside for later." Ordinary savings are built, at least in part, for exactly this kind of situation — a disruption that needs bridging in the near term. Retirement accounts, particularly tax-advantaged ones, are built for a much longer horizon, and accessing them early frequently comes with a real, calculable cost: a penalty, a tax consequence, or a permanent reduction in compounding growth that a household won't fully feel for years, which makes it easy to underweight in a moment when the more immediate, visible costs of the gap are commanding most of the attention.

Pausing contributions before considering withdrawals

For most households, the more urgent and less costly decision isn't whether to withdraw from a retirement account, it's whether to pause new contributions to one during the gap itself, freeing up that portion of income for the more immediate Load covered in Part Three. This is a considerably lower-cost decision than an early withdrawal in most cases, particularly for a household that expects a return to contributing once income resumes, and it's worth treating as the first lever to consider in this category before a withdrawal even enters the conversation. Wendell paused his retirement contributions entirely for the four months his gap ran past his original estimate, resuming them the month his new position began, without ever needing to consider an early withdrawal at all.

What to actually calculate before withdrawing early

If pausing contributions and every other option covered elsewhere in this book genuinely isn't enough, and an early withdrawal is under real consideration, it's worth calculating the actual, specific cost before deciding — not a general sense that early withdrawals are expensive, but the real numbers for your specific account and jurisdiction: what percentage is lost to penalty, what the tax treatment actually looks like, and what that amount would likely have grown to by the time it was originally intended to be used. This calculation is specific enough, and consequential enough, that it deserves a conversation with a qualified financial or tax professional familiar with your particular accounts, rather than a decision made from a general rule of thumb in a book that can't see your specific plan or jurisdiction.

Employer matching, and what pausing contributions actually costs

For a household still employed but facing reduced income — a partner who's had hours cut, for instance, even while remaining employed — it's worth factoring in whether an employer match is tied to ongoing contributions, since pausing entirely might mean forgoing free matching funds, not just the household's own contribution. In some cases, reducing a contribution percentage rather than pausing it completely preserves at least a portion of an employer match while still freeing up meaningful cash flow — worth checking directly with your plan's specific rules before assuming pausing entirely is the only option.

What "not to sacrifice" actually means here

The chapter title's phrase is deliberate: this isn't a chapter arguing that retirement savings should never be touched under any circumstances, since for some households in a genuinely severe gap, a partial early withdrawal is a reasonable, informed choice among a set of imperfect options. It's a chapter arguing for treating this specific category of savings with more deliberation than a bill you can renegotiate or a subscription you can pause, precisely because the cost of an early withdrawal is real, calculable, and easy to underweight in the moment — and because Chapter Sixteen's decision-fatigue warning applies with particular force here, where a tired household might reach for the account that's easiest to access rather than the one that costs least to actually use.

Reassessing once income returns

Chapter Twenty-Three's return-of-income work applies directly here too: once income resumes, resuming contributions at their previous level — or, if a withdrawal was necessary, building a specific plan to replace what was taken, distinct from ordinary reserve-rebuilding — deserves its own explicit line in the household's post-gap budget, rather than being left to happen automatically over an unspecified future stretch of time.

Self-employed households and retirement savings without an employer plan

For a household like Tobias's, where retirement savings were never tied to an employer plan in the first place, this chapter's core questions still apply, just without the employer-match consideration — the decision is simply between continuing regular contributions to a personal retirement account and redirecting that money toward the more immediate Load covered in Part Three. Tobias chose to pause his own contributions entirely during his gap, a more straightforward decision without a match to weigh, and treated resuming them as one of the first things he did once his income stabilized again, using the same explicit, budgeted-line approach Chapter Twenty-Three recommends for any household resuming a paused financial habit once the gap has closed.

When only one partner's income included a retirement plan

In a household where only the partner who lost income had access to an employer retirement plan, the decision about pausing contributions is more straightforward, since there's no ongoing plan to weigh mid-gap — but it's worth a specific note that the household's overall retirement savings rate has genuinely dropped, not just paused temporarily and invisibly, and deserves the same deliberate resumption treatment described above once income returns, rather than being quietly absorbed into "things are back to normal" without a specific plan to actually restore the household's prior savings rate.

A brief word on other long-term goals

Everything in this chapter about retirement accounts applies in a lighter form to other long-term savings goals a household may be pursuing — a dedicated education fund, a planned home renovation, a long-term travel goal. None of these carry the same tax and penalty considerations retirement accounts often do, but they deserve the same deliberate treatment rather than either automatic protection or automatic sacrifice: a brief, honest conversation about which goals can pause without real cost, and which, if any, matter enough to the household to protect even during a gap, made consciously rather than by default.

This Week's Crossing

- If you haven't already, decide deliberately whether to pause retirement contributions during the gap, rather than letting the decision happen by default or by oversight.
- If an early withdrawal is under real consideration, calculate the specific penalty, tax cost, and lost future growth for your actual account before deciding, ideally with a qualified professional.
- Check whether your employer match is tied to your contribution level, and factor that into whether pausing fully or reducing partially makes more sense for your household.

Chapter 21: Crossing Alone: The Solo Household

Much of this book's Crossing work assumes at least two adults sharing the weight of a gap — a partner to have the foundational conversation from Chapter Eight with, a second set of hands to divide the practical work between. A meaningful number of households facing an income gap are single-adult households, whether by circumstance or by household structure, and the crossing looks different when there's no built-in partner to share it with day to day. This chapter is for that household specifically — for readers like Ruth and Tobias, whose gaps this book has followed from the beginning, crossing largely on their own.

Why "alone" doesn't have to mean "unsupported"

The absence of a live-in partner doesn't mean the absence of a support system, even though it can feel that way in the early, disorienting days of a gap, when the instinct to handle everything privately runs especially strong for someone without a built-in household partner to process it with out loud. The Crossing category from Chapter Four still applies fully to a solo household — it simply draws its support from a different, more deliberately assembled network: close friends, extended family, a former colleague, a sibling, rather than a partner sharing the same address. Chapter Fourteen's honest, bounded disclosure work matters more, not less, for a solo household, since it's often the primary mechanism by which practical support and companionship in the process arrive at all.

Building a deliberate support structure, since it won't assemble itself

A partnered household often has its foundational money conversation somewhat naturally, prompted by simply living in the same space. A solo household benefits from being more deliberate about creating an equivalent structure, since it doesn't happen automatically. This might mean identifying one or two specific people — a sibling, a close friend, a former colleague — and asking them directly to be a regular sounding board during the gap, effectively standing in for some of the Crossing function a partner would otherwise provide. Ruth asked a close friend from a previous job, a few weeks into her search, if she'd be willing to have a standing biweekly call specifically to talk through how the search and the finances were going — a small, deliberate request that gave her something closer to the shared-processing benefit Chapter Eight describes for partnered households, built intentionally rather than assumed.

The Bridge Reading, solo

The Bridge Reading from Chapter Fifteen works perfectly well as a solo practice, and if anything, the discipline of keeping it on a fixed schedule matters more for a household without a partner's presence serving as a natural, ambient check on the numbers. Tobias found that doing his Bridge Reading out loud, even alone — literally speaking the five checkpoints aloud rather than only reviewing them silently — made the practice feel less like a private worry spiral and more like the same structured, bounded check-in described throughout this book, a small technique worth trying for any solo reader who finds the practice starting to drift toward rumination rather than a clear fifteen-minute process.

Watching for isolation, specifically

A solo household facing a genuine income gap carries a specific risk that's worth naming directly: the same instinct toward privacy that can make disclosure feel harder, covered in Chapter Fourteen, combines with the simple absence of another adult in the home to create real potential for isolation during an already difficult stretch. This is worth watching for actively rather than assuming it will resolve on its own — scheduling regular, non-negotiable contact with other people, even briefly, matters as much for wellbeing during a solo gap as any of the financial mechanics covered elsewhere in this book, and it's reasonable to treat it as its own deliberate line item rather than something that happens automatically.

Housing and coverage decisions without a second income to weigh

The housing chapter's calculations from Chapter Twelve and the coverage work from Chapter Thirteen apply the same way to a solo household, though the margin for error is often narrower, since there's no second income providing any cushion at all against a miscalculation. This isn't a reason for extra alarm — it's a reason for the same careful, deliberate approach this book asks of every household, applied with perhaps slightly more attention to the Footings and Span work in Chapters One through Three and Chapter Seven, since a solo household's actual numbers deserve to be gotten right the first time rather than adjusted later under more pressure.

What Tobias and Ruth would both tell you

Both Ruth and Tobias, looking back on their own gaps, named the same specific lesson independently: the parts of this book's method that felt least necessary to a solo household at first — the deliberate disclosure work, the scheduled support calls, the discipline of a fixed Bridge Reading rhythm — turned out to matter as much as, or more than, the purely financial mechanics, precisely because they were the pieces actively working against the isolation a solo gap can otherwise produce.

Solo parents specifically

A solo household that also includes children carries a particular version of this chapter's challenge: the isolation risk described above, combined with the full weight of Chapter Nine's routine-protection and honest-conversation work, with no second adult in the home to share either task with day to day. This combination deserves real acknowledgment rather than a brisk "you're managing two chapters' worth of work at once, so just do both" — it's worth being especially deliberate about the support network described earlier in this chapter, since a solo parent's support system is doing double duty: providing the adult companionship a partner might otherwise offer, and, ideally, occasionally providing genuine practical help with the children themselves, even briefly, so the parent gets a small, regular window of the kind of individual space that's much harder to come by in a solo-parent household than in almost any other configuration this book describes.

When family lives nearby but isn't a natural first call

Some solo households have family relatively nearby that, for reasons of history or temperament, isn't the first or easiest source of support to draw on — a parent who reacts with more anxiety than help, a sibling relationship that isn't close in the way this chapter's suggestions assume. If that's your situation, the deliberate-construction advice above matters even more, not less: build your support structure from the relationships that actually function well for you, whatever their category, rather than defaulting to family simply because they're geographically close or technically available.

This Week's Crossing

- Identify one or two specific people to ask directly for a regular, standing check-in during your gap, rather than waiting for support to arrive unprompted.
- Try running your next Bridge Reading out loud, even alone, if the practice has started to feel more like private worry than a structured check.
- Schedule one piece of non-negotiable social contact this week that has nothing to do with the gap itself.

Chapter 22: Debt Collectors, Credit Scores, and Protecting What You've Built

For a household whose income gap runs long enough, or whose starting position was tight enough, a specific new category of concern eventually enters the picture: a payment that does end up missed despite the renegotiation efforts in Chapter Six, a call from a collections department, or a growing worry about what a stretch of financial strain will do to a credit history built up over years. This chapter addresses that territory directly and calmly, since fear in this specific area tends to run considerably ahead of the actual, manageable reality for most households.

What a missed payment actually does, and doesn't, mean

A single missed payment, especially one addressed proactively through the renegotiation approach from Chapter Six, is rarely the catastrophic, irreversible event it can feel like in the moment. Most creditors have some tolerance built into their reporting timelines, and many hardship arrangements, negotiated in advance, prevent a payment from being reported as missed at all, even when the amount or timing has been adjusted from the original terms. The genuinely damaging pattern is a payment missed silently, with no contact and no arrangement in place, repeated over several months — which is exactly the scenario the proactive approach throughout this book is designed to prevent in the first place.

Understanding a collections call before responding to it

If a collections call does arrive, it helps considerably to know a few basic facts before responding to it in the moment, rather than reacting purely from the anxiety the call itself tends to produce. In most jurisdictions, you have a right to request written verification of a debt before making any payment or agreement, a right to request that contact happen in writing rather than by repeated phone calls if that's your preference, and a right to take time to review any proposed arrangement rather than agreeing to something on the spot during an unexpected call. None of this is about avoiding a legitimate debt — it's about responding to it from a position of informed calm rather than pressured urgency, which consistently produces better outcomes and fewer regretted agreements.

A simple script for a collections conversation

A short, calm structure works well here, similar in spirit to the renegotiation script from Chapter Six: acknowledge the contact without agreeing to anything immediately, request written verification of the debt and any proposed arrangement, and take the conversation offline to review before committing. Something like: "I want to address this, and I'd like to see the details in writing before we discuss a specific arrangement — can you send that over, and I'll follow up within a few days?" This isn't evasive; it's a reasonable, standard request that any legitimate collector should be able to accommodate, and it protects you from agreeing, under pressure, to terms that don't actually fit your household's real Span and Load.

Protecting a credit history during a longer gap

For households in a longer gap, particularly the kind covered in Chapter Sixteen, it's worth being deliberate about which payments matter most to protect, since not every account carries equal weight for a credit history. Payments on accounts that report to credit bureaus — most credit cards, loans, and mortgages — generally deserve priority over accounts that don't report at all, when a genuine choice has to be made about which payment gets made first in a particularly tight week. This isn't a universal ranking that overrides every other consideration in this book, but it's a useful additional factor worth weighing alongside the essential-versus-discretionary sorting from Chapter Five when a real tradeoff has to be made.

When professional help is worth bringing in

For a household facing genuinely serious debt strain — multiple accounts in collections, a level of debt that renegotiation alone clearly isn't going to resolve — a nonprofit credit counseling service, distinct from a for-profit debt-settlement company, is worth investigating directly. Reputable credit counseling organizations typically offer free or low-cost initial consultations and can help build a structured repayment plan that a household working alone might not have access to. This is a meaningfully different category of support than anything else in this book, and it's worth seeking out specifically rather than trying to solve a genuinely serious debt situation using only the general tools covered elsewhere in these chapters.

Keeping this in proportion

For most households working through the method in this book — building the inventory in Chapter Five, renegotiating proactively in Chapter Six, mapping the real runway in Chapter

Seven — this chapter's territory never becomes more than a background concern that's addressed calmly if it arises at all. It's included here specifically for the households who do encounter it, so that if a collections call comes or a missed payment happens despite genuine effort, it arrives as a known, manageable situation rather than an unfamiliar crisis on top of an already difficult stretch.

A word of caution about debt-settlement offers

Households showing visible signs of financial strain sometimes become targets for for-profit debt-settlement companies, distinct from the nonprofit credit counseling organizations mentioned above, whose offers can sound similar on the surface but carry real risks — significant fees, advice to stop paying creditors entirely while funds accumulate in a settlement account, and potential damage to a credit history that can outlast whatever short-term relief the arrangement provides. It's worth knowing the difference before responding to either kind of offer: a reputable nonprofit credit counselor typically charges little or nothing for an initial consultation and won't ask you to stop paying your creditors as a first step, while a for-profit settlement company's business model often depends on exactly that.

Which debts to prioritize when a real tradeoff exists

Beyond the credit-reporting consideration mentioned above, it's generally worth prioritizing secured debt — a mortgage or an auto loan, where the lender can repossess the underlying asset — ahead of unsecured debt like most credit cards, where the consequences of a missed payment, while real, don't include losing your home or your vehicle. This isn't a rule that overrides every other factor in this book, particularly interest rate, but it's a useful additional lens when a genuine, narrow tradeoff has to be made in a single tight week between two payments that can't both be made in full.

This Week's Crossing

- If you're facing a missed payment, contact the creditor proactively using Chapter Six's approach before it's reported, rather than waiting for a collections call to happen first.
- If a collections call does arrive, use the calm script here — acknowledge, request written verification, take time before agreeing to anything.
- If debt strain feels genuinely serious rather than manageable through renegotiation alone, look into a reputable nonprofit credit counseling service this week.

~

PART FIVE: REACHING THE FAR BANK

~

Chapter 23: When Income Returns

The day a household's second income actually returns rarely feels the way anyone expected it to during the gap itself. Most households, at some point during a difficult stretch, imagine the return of income as a clean, immediate return to relief — and the reality, for most, is more complicated: a mix of genuine relief, an unfamiliar disorientation about how to spend or save again, and sometimes a strange, unexpected grief for a version of household management that, whatever its stress, had also become oddly familiar. This chapter is about handling that specific transition well, since a poorly managed return can undo some of the genuine gains a household built during the gap itself.

Why the return isn't simply "reverse the gap"

There's a natural assumption that once income returns, a household can simply reverse whatever changes it made during the gap and resume exactly where it left off. This assumption undersells both the real financial position most households are actually in — often, at minimum, a reduced savings buffer that takes time to rebuild — and the real changes that happened over the course of the gap, some of which are worth keeping deliberately rather than discarding automatically. Naomi and Theo, once Theo's new position began, found themselves tempted to immediately restore every subscription and spending habit they'd paused, and paused instead, deliberately, to ask which of those pauses had actually been worth keeping regardless of income — a smaller number turned out to be truly missed than either of them had expected going in.

Rebuilding what was drawn down, deliberately and in order

If savings were drawn down during the gap, following Chapter Ten's order of operations, rebuilding them deserves the same deliberate approach rather than an assumption that it will happen automatically now that income has returned. A useful starting point is treating reserve rebuilding as its own line item in the household's post-gap budget, with a specific, modest monthly target, rather than leaving it to whatever happens to be left over after every other spending decision — the same mistake, in reverse, that let discretionary spending crowd out saving before the gap ever began for some households.

Deciding what to keep from the gap, and what to let go

Some of what a household builds during an income gap is worth carrying forward permanently, and some of it was appropriately temporary and can be released without any sense of loss. The Bridge Reading rhythm from Chapter Fifteen, in particular, is worth strong consideration for keeping in some form even after income returns — many households that adopt a regular, brief financial check-in during a crisis find real, lasting value in continuing a lighter version of it afterward, since it was never really about the gap specifically, it was about a household staying in shared, accurate contact with its own numbers. Other changes — an aggressively reduced grocery budget, a paused activity a child genuinely missed — are appropriate to release fully once the underlying need for them has passed.

Managing the emotional reset, not just the financial one

The financial reset gets most of the practical attention, but the emotional one deserves its own acknowledgment. A period of genuine strain, successfully worked through, often leaves both relief and a kind of residual vigilance that doesn't disappear the moment a new paycheque arrives — an instinct to keep bracing that takes real, conscious effort to stand down from. This is a normal response to having gotten through something truly hard, not a sign that anything is wrong, and it's worth naming directly with a partner or within the household rather than letting it linger unspoken, particularly since Chapter Seventeen's differing-response patterns can resurface here too, with one partner ready to relax sooner than the other.

Zoe and Malik's return, six weeks after moving back into their own place

Zoe and Malik's gap ended when Malik accepted a new position roughly eleven weeks after his layoff, and their own housing situation — having spent six weeks living with Zoe's sister, as covered in Chapter Twelve — added its own layer to the transition, since moving back into their own place happened around the same time as income returning, doubling up two significant changes in a short window. They found it actually helpful to slow that transition down deliberately rather than rushing to restore every piece of their old life simultaneously, giving both changes — the housing return and the income return — their own space rather than treating the whole thing as a single event to get through as fast as possible.

Sharing the good news with the same honesty as the bad

Chapter Fourteen's advice about honest, bounded disclosure applies just as much to good news as to the original announcement of the gap — the people who heard an honest, specific update about the loss generally appreciate an equally honest, specific update about its resolution, rather than being left to piece together that things have improved from secondhand mentions or a return to normal social patterns. This isn't just good manners; it closes the loop on relationships that may have offered real support during the gap, and it models, for anyone in your network who might face a similar gap someday, that this kind of disruption really can resolve well, which is exactly the kind of specific, credible reassurance Chapter Fourteen noted that vague updates rarely provide.

The first paycheque back, and the urge to celebrate hard

There's a strong, understandable pull toward marking the return of income with a significant celebration — a nice dinner out, a purchase that had been deferred for months, some tangible signal that the hard stretch is genuinely over. A modest version of this is worth allowing, consistent with Chapter Sixteen's point about protecting morale as real, legitimate spending rather than pure indulgence. The distinction worth holding onto is scale: a small, deliberate celebration fits comfortably alongside the reserve-rebuilding work described above; a large one, funded by treating the first paycheque as if the household's financial position has already fully recovered, tends to undercut the very stability that paycheque is meant to help rebuild.

A final word on timing that feels unfair

Occasionally, income returns at a moment that feels poorly timed in its own way — a new position starting the same week as an unrelated household expense, an offer arriving after a household has already made a significant, hard-to-reverse decision it might have made differently with more notice. This is worth naming honestly rather than pretending the relief of income returning erases every other complication instantly. Both things can be true at once: genuine relief that the gap has closed, and genuine frustration at its specific timing. Making room for both, rather than feeling obligated to perform pure gratitude the moment income resumes, tends to produce a more honest and ultimately smoother transition.

This Week's Crossing

- If income has recently returned, hold off on automatically restoring every paused expense, and instead review which pauses are worth keeping deliberately.
- Set a specific, modest monthly target for rebuilding any savings drawn down during the gap, and treat it as its own budget line rather than an afterthought.
- Name the emotional reset directly with your household — the instinct to keep bracing even after the practical situation has resolved — rather than letting it go unspoken.

Chapter 24: Build the Buffer for Next Time

An income gap, once it's over, tends to teach a household something specific and durable about its own finances that no amount of general advice could have taught nearly as effectively in advance — exactly where its real flexibility lives, exactly which fixed costs turned out to be genuinely fixed and which had more give than assumed, exactly how long its reserves actually lasted against real spending rather than a theoretical projection. This chapter is about converting those hard-won, specific lessons into a durable system, so that if a household ever faces another gap, it crosses it from a meaningfully stronger position than it did this time.

Turning the gap into data, not just an experience

Most households, once a gap ends, are eager to move past it and avoid revisiting it in detail, which is an understandable instinct and also a missed opportunity, since the gap just lived through contains genuinely useful information a household won't have access to again until, potentially, the next one. Setting aside even a single hour, once things have settled, to review what actually happened — how long the gap really lasted against the original timeline range from Chapter Three, which bill renegotiations from Chapter Six actually mattered most, how the runway calculation from Chapter Seven compared to reality — turns a difficult experience into a specific, usable reference for the future, distinct from a vague memory of "that was a hard few months."

Setting a reserve target based on real experience, not a generic rule

General financial advice often recommends a reserve sized to a fixed number of months of expenses, based on broad averages rather than any specific household's actual situation. A household that has just been through a real gap has something more useful available: an actual data point for how long its own gap lasted, and an actual sense of which costs proved essential versus flexible under real pressure. Wendell used his own five-month gap, once it ended, to set a reserve target meaningfully larger than the generic three-month rule he'd followed loosely before — not out of anxiety, but because he now had real information suggesting his own household's realistic exposure ran longer than that generic guideline had assumed.

Building the reserve without recreating the strain that just ended

It's worth being deliberate about the pace of reserve-building after a gap, since an aggressive, high-pressure savings push right after a period of real financial strain can recreate some of the same tension the household just worked hard to move past, without the same underlying urgency to justify it. A steady, modest, sustainable contribution — treated the way Chapter Ten treated pre-gap savings, as a real budget line rather than whatever's left over — tends to actually stick over the following months and years, where an intense short-term push followed by burnout on the whole practice often doesn't.

Keeping a version of the inventory and the scripts on hand

The bill inventory from Chapter Five and the renegotiation approach from Chapter Six don't need to be rebuilt from scratch if a future gap ever arrives — keeping a simple, occasionally updated version of both on hand, even during ordinary times when no gap is underway, means a household facing a future disruption starts from a running head start rather than the same blank page it started from this time. This doesn't need to be elaborate. A single document, reviewed once or twice a year during an otherwise unrelated Bridge Reading, keeps this information current without requiring ongoing active attention.

What carries forward relationally, not just financially

The Crossing work from Part Three — the partner conversations from Chapter Eight, the honest disclosure practice from Chapter Fourteen, the recognition of differing response styles from Chapter Seventeen — is worth carrying forward as deliberately as the financial lessons, since a household that has now come through one real gap together has genuine, hard-won practice at exactly the kind of communication that made this one more manageable. Naming that explicitly, as something the household is now better at rather than something that simply happened and is now over, helps it stay available the next time it's needed, rather than fading the way a difficult memory that isn't actively maintained tends to.

A buffer is not a guarantee, and that's fine

None of this converts a household into one that can never be caught off guard again — an income gap is, by definition, largely outside a household's control, and no amount of preparation eliminates that. What a rebuilt reserve, a maintained inventory, and a practiced set of Crossing skills actually offer is a shorter, less strained version of the same gap, should one ever arrive again — a narrower distance to cross, with a sturdier bridge already partly built, rather than starting entirely from the ground up the way this gap likely did.

Telling kids what changed, once it's over

Chapter Nine covered how to talk with children during the gap itself; it's worth a brief, honest follow-up conversation once the gap has closed and the buffer-building work in this chapter is underway. Children who were told, accurately, that a routine or a decision was temporary benefit from hearing, just as clearly, that the household made it through and is now taking steps to be ready if something similar happens again — a short conversation that reinforces exactly the kind of durable confidence this chapter describes at the household level, translated into terms a child can hold onto. Naomi and Theo's kids, months after the gap had closed, still occasionally mention "the bridge fund" — their own child-invented name for the family's rebuilt reserve — a small sign that the lesson had genuinely landed, not just for the adults.

A written record worth keeping past this gap

The one-hour review described above is worth writing down in some durable form, not just discussing out loud, since memory of a difficult stretch tends to soften or distort over the following years in ways that make the specific, useful lessons harder to recall accurately when they'd actually be needed again. A single page — how long the gap actually ran, what the true monthly burn looked like once triage math gave way to real figures, which specific renegotiations produced the largest savings — kept alongside the workbook in this book's appendix, gives a future version of your household a concrete, specific reference rather than a vague sense that "we got through something hard once."

This Week's Crossing

- Spend one hour reviewing what actually happened during your gap, comparing your real timeline and real numbers against your original estimates.
- Set a reserve target based on your own household's real experience rather than a generic rule of thumb, and build toward it at a steady, sustainable pace.
- Save a simple, current version of your bill inventory and renegotiation notes somewhere you'll actually find them again, for a possible future gap.

Chapter 25: The Household That Crossed Together

There's a particular kind of household confidence that only comes from having actually crossed a real gap, together, and come out the other side with the relationship and the finances both intact — a confidence no amount of reading about the possibility of an income loss can produce in advance, and one that's worth naming clearly as this book closes, because it's easy to underestimate what it actually means until you're standing on the far side of it.

A last word on the word "successfully"

This book has occasionally used the phrase "handled well" or "come through successfully" to describe a household's crossing, and it's worth being precise about what that actually means, since it isn't a claim that the crossing was easy, painless, or free of real fear along the way. Every household in these pages felt genuine strain at some point in their gap — Naomi's static on the first day, Ruth's uncomfortable evening mistaking a rough triage number for a verdict on her worth, Corinne and Dev's early disagreement about how much to tell her mother. A successful crossing, in this book's terms, was never about avoiding those moments. It was about having a method sturdy enough to hold them, and a process to return to once the moment had passed.

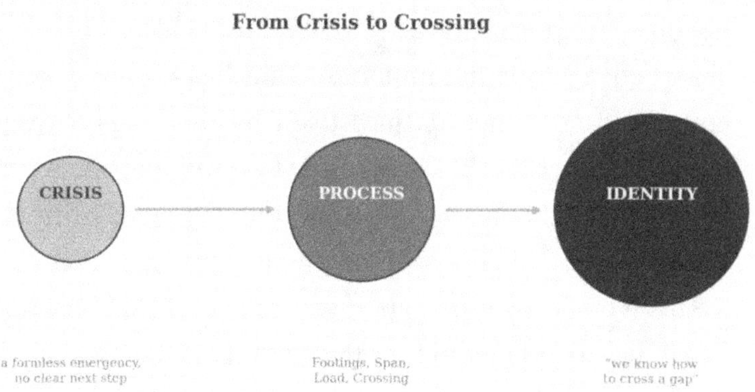

From crisis to crossing: how a formless emergency becomes a practiced process, and eventually an identity.

What changes, once a household has done this once

A household that has come through a genuine, unchosen income gap using a deliberate method, rather than pure improvisation, tends to carry forward something more durable than an updated spreadsheet or a rebuilt reserve, though both of those matter too. It carries forward a working knowledge of its own resilience — a concrete, specific memory of having faced a real disruption and handled it, together, using a clear process rather than panic. That knowledge tends to quietly reduce the background anxiety many households carry about financial uncertainty generally, not because the risk of a future disruption has gone away, but because the household now has direct evidence that it can meet that risk capably if it arrives.

The identity shift, from "a household in crisis" to "a household that knows how to cross"

Early in a gap, most households experience themselves primarily through the lens of the disruption itself — the layoff, the uncertainty, the strain. By the time a gap has resolved and the lessons from Chapter Twenty-Four have been genuinely absorbed, a subtle but important shift has usually taken place: the household no longer defines itself by the crisis it went through, but by the fact that it knows how to build and use a bridge when one is needed. This is the same identity-level shift that shapes lasting change in almost any domain — the goal was never simply to survive one specific gap, it was to become a household that has a real, practiced method for the version of this that any household might eventually face.

What this book was actually teaching, underneath the tactics

Every specific tactic in this book — the triage math, the renegotiation scripts, the bill inventory, the Bridge Reading rhythm — serves a single underlying purpose that's worth stating plainly now that the full method has been laid out: replacing panic with a process. Panic treats an income gap as a formless emergency requiring maximum, undirected effort in every direction at once. A process treats it as a specific, bounded problem with a known shape — Footings, Span, Load, Crossing — that can be worked through deliberately, checked regularly, and adjusted as needed, without pretending the situation isn't hard, and without letting its difficulty produce chaos instead of clarity.

Carrying the mantra forward, even in calmer times

Bridge, not blueprint applies well beyond the specific situation of an income gap, and many households that have internalized it during a genuine crisis find it useful more broadly afterward, for other bounded, uncertain stretches life tends to produce — a health scare, a difficult stretch with an aging parent, any period defined by real but likely temporary strain. The instinct to build something sized to the actual, current distance, rather than either freezing in place or overbuilding for a permanent future that may never arrive, turns out to be a genuinely durable piece of household wisdom, not a tactic that expires the moment this specific gap closes.

A closing word for whoever is reading this in the middle of their own gap

If you're reading this final chapter already on the other side of your own income gap, the households throughout this book — and the six behind their composite names, explained fully in the note that follows — hope something here made the crossing steadier than it would have been otherwise. If you're reading this chapter while still in the middle of your own gap, hoping to understand where the road eventually leads: it leads here, to a shorter chapter than most in this book, because by the time a household reaches this page in its own life, there's usually less left to explain and more simply to live. The bridge holds. Keep crossing.

What to tell the next household you meet

At some point after a gap closes, most people eventually meet someone else standing where they once stood — a colleague whose position was just eliminated, a friend whose partner's contract just ended, a neighbor who mentions, carefully, that things have gotten uncertain at home. That moment is worth taking seriously rather than letting pass with a generic "I'm sure it'll work out." You now have something more useful than sympathy to offer: a specific, lived account of what actually helped, which questions actually mattered, and which fears turned out to be larger than the reality. Ruth, once her own search ended, became the person a former colleague called eighteen months later when his own layoff arrived — not because she'd become an expert in any formal sense, but because she was willing to say plainly what had worked and what hadn't, rather than offering only comfort. Passing that on, deliberately, is its own small way of keeping the bridge you built useful beyond your own crossing.

This Week's Crossing

- Name, out loud with your household if you've reached the other side of a gap, what you now know about your own resilience that you didn't know before.
- Identify one other kind of bounded, uncertain stretch in life where "bridge, not blueprint" might serve you as well as it did here.
- If you're still mid-crossing, return to whichever chapter in this book matches exactly where you are today, and do this week's version of the work — one small piece at a time is still how every household in these pages got across.

APPENDIX

The Household Bridge Workbook

The chapters in this book each end with a short "This Week's Crossing" list, sized to be done in the middle of an already difficult week. This appendix gathers the core calculations and checklists referenced throughout the book into one place, so that a household can return to them directly — during the first triage in Chapter Two, during a Bridge Reading in Chapter Fifteen, or at any later point — without hunting back through earlier chapters to find the right worksheet. Photocopy these pages, recreate them in a notebook or a shared document, or simply use them as a template for your own version. None of them need to be filled out perfectly, and none of them need to be filled out all at once.

Worksheet One: The Forty-Eight-Hour Triage Number

This is the calculation from Chapter Two, meant to be completed quickly, using rough figures rather than perfect ones.

Figure	Amount
Cash on hand (chequing and savings combined)	
Committed monthly outflow (housing, debt, insurance, utilities)	
Confirmed incoming money (final pay, severance, benefits)	
Estimated weeks of runway	

Worksheet Two: The Five-Category Bill Inventory

Use this to build the complete inventory from Chapter Five. List every recurring cost, then mark it Fixed, Negotiable, or Removable.

Bill	Category	Amount	Flexibility

Worksheet Three: The Severance and Benefits Calendar

Use this to build the week-by-week map from Chapter Seven. List every confirmed source of income or support against the week it actually arrives.

Week Number	Source	Expected Amount	Confirmed?

Week Number	Source	Expected Amount	Confirmed?

Worksheet Four: The Renegotiation Call Log

Use this to track the calls from Chapter Six as you make them, so nothing gets lost between conversations.

Provider	Date Called	Outcome	Confirmed in Writing?

Worksheet Five: The Bridge Reading Checklist

Use this every time you sit down for the fifteen-minute check described in Chapter Fifteen. The same five checkpoints, every time.

Checkpoint	This Reading	Compared to Last Reading
Runway (weeks)		
Bill inventory changes		
Timeline range		
Coverage status		
One thing working / one to adjust		

Worksheet Six: The Household Conversation Starter

Use this before your first shared money conversation, described in Chapter Eight. Each adult in the household fills this out separately, then compares answers together.

Question	Your Answer
What do I fear most about this situation?	
What would help me feel like we're handling this well?	
What's one thing I don't want to change, if possible?	
What's one thing I'm genuinely willing to change?	

Worksheet Seven: The Housing Decision Comparison

Use this alongside Chapter Twelve when weighing whether to stay, downsize, or share housing. Fill in your best honest estimate for each option, including the one-time costs of changing, not just the ongoing monthly difference.

Factor	Stay	Downsize	Share
Monthly housing cost			
One-time cost to change			
Months to recoup that cost			
Impact on kids' routines			

Worksheet Eight: The Network Disclosure List

Use this alongside Chapter Fourteen to plan honest, bounded disclosure deliberately rather than leaving it to chance encounters and awkward half-updates.

Name	Relationship	What I'll Tell Them	Specific Ask

Name	Relationship	What I'll Tell Them	Specific Ask

Using this workbook as the gap continues

Most households find these six worksheets cover the vast majority of what comes up across a typical gap, from the first frantic hour to the calmer, more routine stretch of monthly Bridge Readings described in Chapter Fifteen. It's worth keeping this workbook, or your own version of it, in one consistent place — a single notebook, a shared folder, a specific tab in a phone's notes app — so that updating it becomes part of the fifteen-minute rhythm rather than a separate search each time. A household that keeps this workbook current through the whole gap, as Chapter Twenty-Four discusses, ends up with a genuinely useful record once the gap closes: not just a memory of a hard stretch, but a specific, concrete account of exactly how it was handled, ready to be referenced again if it's ever needed.

~

BACK MATTER

~

About the Author

Felix N.BBA.MA. is a real estate investor, spiritual leader, serial entrepreneur, author, and strategic advisor whose career spans founding businesses, government work, and real estate investing across Europe, Africa, the Americas, and beyond. He helps leaders and aspiring professionals build success using strategies rooted in manifestation, spirituality, and business psychology. As the author of several transformative books, Felix N.BBA.MA. shares practical insights that help readers unlock wealth, elevate their mindset, and create lasting impact.

Disclaimer

This book is intended for general informational and educational purposes only. It does not constitute financial, legal, tax, insurance, credit, or professional advice, and nothing in these pages should be treated as a substitute for consultation with a qualified professional familiar with your household's specific circumstances and jurisdiction.

The strategies, frameworks, and examples described are shared in good faith based on the author's experience and perspective. They are not a guarantee of any particular financial outcome, and results will vary by household, region, employer, and circumstance. Programs, protections, and coverage options referenced in general terms — including income support, benefit continuation, and debt-related protections — vary considerably by country and region, and readers should confirm what actually applies to them with the relevant institution or a qualified professional rather than relying on this book alone. Any decision to apply the ideas in this book — including decisions about savings, debt, housing, coverage, or credit — remains the reader's own responsibility, made in consultation with appropriate professionals where needed.

As explained in "A Note on the Households in These Pages," the households and case examples referenced throughout this book are composites and are not intended to represent any specific, identifiable person or family.

The author and publisher disclaim liability for any loss or risk, personal or otherwise, incurred as a direct or indirect consequence of the use or application of any of the material in this book.

A Note on the Households in These Pages

Naomi and Theo, Imani and Sam, Ruth, Tobias, Zoe and Malik, and Corinne and Dev are composites. None of them is a single real, identifiable person or family, and none of the specific incidents attached to them — the closed regional office, the parental leave that turned into a longer gap, the corporate restructuring, the ended freelance contract, the six weeks spent living with a sister, the nonprofit position eliminated without severance — is a factual account of one traceable event. They're built from patterns that repeat constantly across households facing an unchosen income gap: the kind of Tuesday-afternoon phone call, the kind of quiet coverage lapse, the kind of overdue honest conversation, that many readers of this book will recognize from their own experience, even though the specific names and details are invented.

This is a deliberate choice, not a shortcut. A genuine case study, detailed enough to be useful, is usually detailed enough to be recognizable to real family members, real employers, and real friends who never agreed to have their hardest months published in a book. Composite households let this book be specific and concrete — which is what makes advice like this usable rather than abstract — without asking anyone's actual crisis to become someone else's chapter title.

If any part of Naomi and Theo's layoff or Ruth's five-month search or Tobias's ended contract feels uncannily close to something that happened in your own household, that's the method working as intended, not a coincidence to be explained. These patterns repeat because an unchosen income gap itself repeats them, across industries, across regions, across the specific year you happen to be reading this in.

Quick Reference: The Bridge Method at a Glance

Keep this page close at hand — on the refrigerator, in a shared notes app, wherever you'd actually look at it during a hard week. It's the entire method compressed to its essentials, for the moments when you don't have time to reread a chapter.

The mantra: Bridge, not blueprint. Build for the actual gap in front of you, sized to the real distance, not a permanent redesign of your household's whole financial life.

Footings. Confirm your triage number, your timeline range, and a temporary pause on discretionary spending, all within the first few days. This is your stable base — get it right before building anything on top of it.

Span. Map every source of income against an actual calendar — severance, benefits, income support, savings — using net figures and real dates, not guesses. Update it as the real distance becomes clearer.

Load. Everything the bridge carries day to day: the bill inventory, the renegotiation calls, the savings order, the housing decision, the coverage check, the bridge-income filter. Handle each piece deliberately, in the order that fits your household.

Crossing. The people making this crossing with you — a partner's differing fears, a child's protected routines, an honest, bounded update to your wider network. None of this book's math matters much if the people carrying it apart from each other.

The Bridge Reading. Fifteen minutes, weekly at first and monthly once things stabilize. Five checkpoints: runway, bill inventory, timeline range, coverage, one thing working and one thing to adjust.

The one test for anything you're tempted to do: does it fit the actual gap in front of you, or does it assume this is either over already or permanent? If it assumes either extreme, hold it loosely until your own numbers say otherwise.

Keep crossing.

A Short Glossary

The Bridge Method. The four-part framework this book uses in place of a rigid financial blueprint: Footings, Span, Load, and Crossing, checked on a recurring rhythm called the Bridge Reading.

Blueprint. A plan built for permanence, assuming a known final shape. The rejected alternative throughout this book — not because permanent planning is wrong in general, but because it's the wrong tool for a gap of unknown, probably temporary width.

Footings. The immediate, non-negotiable stabilization work done in the first days of a gap: the triage number, the timeline range, and an initial pause on discretionary spending.

Span. The measured, mapped distance of the gap itself — every source of income and support plotted against an actual calendar, updated as the real timeline becomes clearer.

Load. Everything the household's plan has to carry day to day: bills, debts, housing, coverage, and income decisions, sorted by what's fixed, negotiable, or removable.

Crossing. The relational work of getting through a gap alongside other people — a partner, children, a wider network — rather than alone, covered in Part Three and revisited in Part Four for households where this strains further than expected.

The Bridge Reading. The recurring fifteen-minute check — weekly at first, monthly once stable — that keeps a household's numbers accurate without requiring one large plan built once and trusted blindly for months.

The in-between. The specific, bounded period this book addresses: the stretch between an unchosen loss of a second income and its eventual return, distinct from both ordinary dual-income budgeting and a deliberately chosen single-income lifestyle.

Composite household. A household in this book — Naomi and Theo, Imani and Sam, Ruth, Tobias, Zoe and Malik, Corinne and Dev — built from repeating patterns across many real households rather than drawn from one specific, identifiable family. See "A Note on the Households in These Pages."

References

The Bridge Method and everything built on it in this book — the four pillars, the Bridge Reading, the composite households and their stories — were developed independently for this book and are not drawn from any single outside source. The titles below are not works this book was built on; they're offered as further reading for readers who want to go deeper into ideas that sit near the ones covered here, from writers working in adjacent territory.

On money and behavior

Housel, Morgan. *The Psychology of Money.* Harriman House, 2020.

On the relationship between money, time, and values

Robin, Vicki, and Joe Dominguez. *Your Money or Your Life.* Penguin, revised edition, 2018.

On the psychology behind financial decisions

Klontz, Brad, and Ted Klontz. *Mind Over Money.* Broadway Books, 2009.

On communication between partners under real strain

Gottman, John M., and Nan Silver. *The Seven Principles for Making Marriage Work.* Harmony, revised edition, 2015.

On career transitions and job searching

Bolles, Richard N. *What Color Is Your Parachute?* Ten Speed Press, annual editions.

On practical, systems-based personal finance

Sethi, Ramit. *I Will Teach You to Be Rich.* Workman, revised edition, 2019.

On building habits that hold up under pressure

Duhigg, Charles. *The Power of Habit.* Random House, 2012.

www.ingramcontent.com/pod-product-compliance
Lightning Source LLC
LaVergne TN
LVHW010726061126
851857LV00014B/1356
9781997156000